CHILDREN OF ONE GOD

CHILDREN OF ONE GOD

A History of the Council of
Christians and Jews

MARCUS BRAYBROOKE

Foreword by Lord Coggan

VALLENTINE MITCHELL

First published in 1991 in Great Britain by
VALLENTINE MITCHELL & CO. LTD
Gainsborough House, Gainsborough Road,
London E11 1RS, England

and in the United States of America by
VALLENTINE MITCHELL
c/o International Specialized Book Services, Inc.
5602 N.E. Hassalo Street, Portland, Oregon 97213

British Library Cataloguing in Publication Data

Braybrooke, Marcus
    Children of one God : a history of
    the Council of Christians and Jews
    I. Title
    200

    ISBN 0 85303 242 4
    ISBN 0 85303 250 5 pbk

Library of Congress Cataloging-in-Publication Data

Braybrooke, Marcus
    Children of one God : a history of the Council of Christians and
Jews / Marcus Braybrooke ; foreword by Lord Coggan.
      p.   cm.
    Includes bibliographical references and index.
    ISBN-0-85303-242-4 : $20.00. — ISBN 0-85303-250-5 (pbk.) : $12.00
    Council of Christians and Jews—History.   2. Christianity and
other religions—Judaism—1945– 3. Judaism—Relations—
Christianity—1945– 4. Jews—Great Britain.   5. Great Britain—
Religion—20th century. I. Title.
BM535.B673 1991
261.2'6'06041—dc20   91-18683
                                                   CIP

Printed and bound in Great Britain by
BPCC Wheatons Ltd, Exeter

The Council of Christians and Jews
gratefully acknowledges
sponsorship from
The Alexander Stone Foundation, Glasgow.

Founder
Dr Alexander Stone, O.B.E.

TO THE MEMORY OF
WILLIAM WYNN SIMPSON, OBE

'I am convinced that the next great phase of the world's history will witness the emergence of a new sense of partnership between the Jewish and Christian worlds, within the kingdom and purpose of God.'

Words of Leo Baeck, shortly before his death

Contents

CONTENTS

8. LOCAL COUNCILS

9. INTERNATIONAL INVOLVEMENT

CONTENTS

List of Illustrations

Grateful acknowledgement is made, where appropriate, of permission to reproduce these photographs.

1. From *In Good Faith*; 2. Hulton-Deutsch; 3. Pamela Gibbs; 4. Sidney Harris; 5. Halifax Photos; 6. Foto Felicia; 8. Jeremy Braybrooke; 9. Times Newspapers Limited; 10. Sidney Harris; 11. John Coghill; 12. The Southport Visiter Series of Newspapers; 13. Sidney Harris.

Foreword

Rt Rev. Lord Coggan, P.C.

Former Archbishop of Canterbury,
former Chairman of CCJ and President of ICCJ

There can be no doubt about the importance of the subject of this book. The relationship between Christians and Jews has been fraught with difficulty from the start of the history of the Church. The story is a sad one, at times a sordid and a tragic one. But there are signs, strong signs, of a break in the clouds, even of some sunshine on the horizon.

It is the purpose of this book to tell of an area in which men and women of goodwill have sought, if not to eradicate the shame of the past (for history cannot be undone), at least to think and plan together, Jews and Christians, on the basis of a faith whose origins are revered in both traditions. The Christian owes the Jew a treasure beyond all price. The days are gone when we 'tolerate' one another. For some decades now, as this book makes clear, we have been 'conferring' together. Some of us believe, with all our hearts, that the time has come when 'toleration' and 'conferring' should lead on to 'cooperation' in a joint approach to a largely godless world, on the basis of what Christians and Jews believe to be a divine revelation both of belief and of ethics.

Was there ever a time when the world needed more than now to hear the prophecy of Micah: 'The Lord has told you mortals what is good, and what it is that the Lord requires of you: only to act justly, to love loyalty, to walk humbly with your God' (6; 8. REB)? Are not Jews and Christians joint trustees of this message to humanity? Has not the time arrived when together they can proclaim it?

Marcus Braybrooke has succeeded in making out of this bit of history a story of real interest, largely because that story is lit up by the action of men and women of vision who have given of themselves and of their money to the furtherance of Christian–Jewish relations. It is a story too little known and too feebly supported –

often the work of the Council of Christians and Jews has been limited and hindered through lack of financial aid. There remains so much to be done, here in Britain and, through the International Council of Christians and Jews, throughout the world.

We owe the author a debt of thanks for writing a book which will alert the attention and stir the consciences of many readers. I wish it well.

Donald Coggan

Preface

I am grateful to all the members of the Council of Christians and Jews, both the anonymous and those mentioned by name, without whom there would have been no history for me to write.

I especially want to thank Lord Coggan, Rev. Dr I. Levy and my wife Mary for reading the script, and Canon Jim Richardson and Rev. Peter Jennings for reading some chapters. Their comments have been very helpful, although I must take responsibility for errors and expressions of opinion.

I appreciate Lord Coggan's encouragement in writing a Foreword.

I owe a great debt to the helpfulness of Dr C.M. Woolgar, the Archivist of the Library at the University of Southampton, for making available papers from the Parkes, CCJ and Simpson archives, to the librarian of the Jewish Chronicle and to the staff of CCJ for providing papers and answering queries. Dr Edward Carpenter generously showed me a chapter from his forthcoming study of Archbishop Fisher. I have also used some of the material which W.W. Simpson had gathered in preparation for the history of CCJ that he had hoped to write. The assistance of Rev. and Mrs Graham Jenkins is gratefully acknowledged.

I also want to thank Margaret Goodare and all at Vallentine Mitchell, who have helped to publish this book so speedily. I am grateful too to those who have made photographs available.

The book has had to be written in three months in the hope that it will be available for the ICCJ Colloquium in Southampton later this year. This has meant that time for background research has been very limited. The book is specifically a history of CCJ and does not attempt to survey the whole field of the changing relationships of Jews and Christians in Britain during this century, although CCJ has made a significant contribution to those changes.

The title, *Children of One God*, does not imply that those of other faiths or of none are not also children of the Holy One. It echoes the first of the ten points of Seelisberg. Sadly, what may seem obvious to some of us has been a costly discovery which many still have to make for themselves.

Fifty years of CCJ is a cause for thanksgiving to God and an occasion for rededication to the work that still needs to be done. Writing this on the day that the Gulf War began, I am only too conscious of how much still needs to be done to develop understanding, cooperation and friendship between all people of faith and good will.

16 January 1991   Marcus Braybrooke

1

Pre-War Preparations

Where to begin? The story could start with the origins of anti-semitism or with the emergence of the Christian church, which so soon became anti-Jewish in outlook and teaching. One could begin with the emancipation or with the resurgence of antisemitism at the end of the nineteenth century, as shown by the pogroms under Czar Alexander III or in the notorious Dreyfus affair in France.

Yet this is not a history of Christian–Jewish relations, only an account of a modest but significant contribution to building under-standing and friendship between Jews and Christians in Britain. The beginnings of the Council of Christians and Jews can be found, therefore, in a number of initiatives taken in Britain during the first half of this century to create understanding between the two religions. Similar developments were also occurring in some other countries, especially the USA, where the National Conference of Christians and Jews was formed in 1928.

EARLY INITIATIVES

From its beginning, the London Society for the Study of Religions included some Jews. The Society was founded in 1904, largely under the inspiration of Baron von Hügel. The most notable Jewish member was the Liberal Jewish scholar Claude Montefiore. He was one of the first members to present a paper, which was on 'A Jewish View of the New Testament'. Between the world wars, the Society often met in his home.

In 1924, at the Presbyterian Church of England Congress, Pro-fessor Elmslie from Cambridge questioned the entire policy of that Church's Jewish Committee. The Committee had been in existence for many years, but its work had dwindled to maintaining two medical missions. One was at Aleppo in Syria, but during the First

1

World War this had virtually ceased to exist. The other was at Bethnal Green. This was not actively conversionist, but gave medical assistance to Jews in the area. Professor Elmslie asked what useful purpose the mission served. A lively debate followed, during which the lack of understanding between Jews and Christians was deplored. It was agreed to form a small committee to meet at Cambridge to discuss the situation.[1]

This sub-committee met in Cambridge on 15 October 1924. Two Jews had been invited, Dr Israel Abrahams and Dr Herbert Loewe, teachers at Cambridge. It seems that those on the committee wished to abandon any conversionist activity and to establish some co-operative action.

The following year, at a meeting of the Jewish Mission Committee, Professor Elmslie spoke sympathetically and appreciatively of Judaism. Then, at the General Assembly, for the first time, a Jew, Herbert Loewe, was invited to speak. He was conscious of the special nature of the occasion. 'I do not know whether such a meeting has been held before. To my mind, it is the Lord's doing, and marvellous in our eyes.' Whilst recognising differences, Herbert Loewe stressed what the two faiths shared.

> The love of God and love of man are the foundations of our Faith and of yours. We have a vast heritage in common. We love the Lord our God with all our hearts, with all our souls, and with all our might. We think alike on so many of the greatest things of life, on truth, charity, justice, peace and brotherhood. We recognise that we are put into this world to serve each other. We believe in a revelation of God in history. We are assured of progress, of the workings of Providence in the government of the world, and we are firmly convinced that mankind gradually but surely is moving forward to a better state of things. When we consider the framework on which our creeds are built the wonder is not that our views of life are similar, but that we should have been so long in discovering the similarity; the wonder is that centuries of ignorance and hatred should have intervened between us, and so tragic a barrier should have hindered our efforts for a common task.

Recognising the differences amongst Jews and amongst Christians, Herbert Loewe went on to say, 'I am convinced that our partnership in the fight against oppression and injustice and race-hatred can never be successful, and our efforts can never be blessed until we learn to respect the standpoint of each other'.[2]

Rev. T.W. Manson, on his induction as the new missionary at Bethnal Green, made clear that the Mission existed solely 'to benefit Jews in every way'. First 'we have to break down those barriers of misunderstanding and dislike which undoubtedly still exist ... Secondly, we are willing to work for and with Jews in anything which serves to help men and women in body, mind or soul.' All this was done as part of the task of proclaiming the Gospel. 'We have found it so good and so true that we want every one, Jews included, to have it.' But Manson rejected any form of pressure; the decision was for the Jews to make, in their relation to God.[3] For a time, the Bethnal Mission became more of a study centre, but eventually the building was destroyed by a bomb during the blitz.

1924 was also the year in which the Social Service Committee of the Liberal Jewish Synagogue felt that 'in spite of serious differences of belief, Jews and Christians were at one in their desire to bring nearer the Kingdom of God on earth'. The Committee, with some other organisations, convened a gathering for 'Jews and Christians to confer together on the basis of their common ideals and with mutual respect for differences of belief'.[4] The Conference on 'Religion as an Educational Force' was held in November 1924. It aroused so much interest that the ad hoc committee was given a more permanent status and eventually, in 1927, a Society of Jews and Christians was established.

The aims of the society, which became known as the London Society for Jews and Christians, were:

1. To increase religious understanding, and to promote goodwill and cooperation between Jews and Christians, with mutual respect for differences of faith and practice.
2. To combat religious intolerance.[5]

The society has had a distinguished history and provided a platform for many well-known speakers. In 1934, a selection of papers was published under the title *In Spirit and in Truth*. In some of these contributions there is a defensive note, because the activities of the society were viewed critically by those suspicious of indifferentism. For example, Hewlett Johnson, who was then Dean of Canterbury, in his introduction, asserted that there was common ground and that Jews and Christians needed each other. But he then made clear

3

that his Christian commitment was not compromised. 'Christianity is the central point in the wide circle of light which shines forth from a heavenly Father ... I long to commend to others what I see.'[6]

SCHOLARS

Another development during the period between the wars was the beginning of a reassessment of Judaism by Christian scholars. In 1930, the first of Dr James Parkes' many contributions to the cause of Jewish–Christian understanding was published. *The Jew and his Neighbour* was a study of the causes of antisemitism, showing the Christian roots of this insidious evil.

James Parkes was brought up in the Channel Islands. After serving in France as an infantry officer during the First World War, he went to Oxford. He then wanted to be ordained as an Anglican clergyman, but objected to the type and quality of examination which was a prerequisite for this. William Temple, however, interceded on his behalf and he was eventually ordained, although he never served as a parish priest. He worked at first with the Student Christian Movement. In 1928 he went to Geneva to take charge of the International Student Service office there. He soon became aware of the rising tide of antisemitism.

In the same year, 1928, that Parkes moved to Geneva, the International Missionary Council held a large conference in Jerusalem. Following this conference, the International Committee on the Christian Approach to the Jews was created as a focal point for all Protestant work related to Jews. Conrad Hoffmann, who had already worked with Jews through the relief work of YMCA (the Young Men's Christian Association), was appointed director. Quickly, Parkes' and Hoffman's different attitudes towards missionary activity became clear. Parkes wrote about this to Hoffmann on 9 December 1930. The Council, Parkes said, implied that

> either one believes in converting the individual Jew when one can, or one does not accept a responsibility for the Jews. Now I do not think you will deny, [Parkes continued] that all the staff of I.S.S. [the International Student Service] try to be Christians, and I think you will also agree that we are accepting our responsibility towards the Jew. But we are, quite definitely, not interested in the evangelisation of the individual

Jew. It seems to me that your brethren have completely left out of account another alternative, which seems to me to be the most truly Christian one at the present time: our Christian responsibility to give the Jew a square deal to be a Jew.[7]

'To give the Jew a square deal to be a Jew' became James Parkes' life's work. 'The absolute basis of my work is that the Jews with whom I am in contact know that I have no secret desire to convert them.'[8] It was to be lonely work, as many in the Churches were critical and many Jews suspicious. He was one of the first to recognise clearly that the root of much antisemitism lay in the teaching of the Churches, as he argued in his doctoral thesis, *The Conflict of Church and Synagogue: A Study in the Origins of Antisemitism*, first published in 1934.

Parkes was, in due course, to be placed on Hitler's 'black list' of those marked out for immediate elimination in the event of a Nazi victory. Already in 1935 he had been a victim of a Nazi attack on his apartment in Geneva. Later that year he came back to Britain and soon settled at Barley, in Hertfordshire, where he devoted himself to scholarly research and writing. His output was prodigious and his *History of the Jewish People* was translated into several languages. On his retirement in 1966, he gave his magnificent library of some 7,000 books and treatises on antisemitism and Christian–Jewish relations to Southampton University.

At Parkes' funeral, Canon Peter Schneider, another pioneer in this field, said, 'It was given to this one man to hew out the foundations, almost with his bare hands and without organisation – and for much of the time without the support of the Church – to create a new relationship between the Church and the Jewish people.'[9] Dr Robert Andrew Everett, in his study of Parkes, says he provided 'a model of a Christian theology able to accept Judaism as an equal'.[10]

His was a lonely task, but there were other pioneers such as Robert Travers Herford (1860–1950), a Unitarian minister and scholar. His many works on the Talmud and Midrash helped to begin a proper Christian appreciation of Rabbinic Judaism and a new less jaundiced view of the Pharisees. George Foot Moore (1851–1931), of Harvard University, also made a massive contribution to these developments. His greatest work was, perhaps, his three-volume *Judaism in the First Centuries of the Christian Era*, published between 1927 and 1930.

THE 1930s

Tragic events on the Continent were soon to demand more than scholarly discussion. Hitler came to power in 1933 and began to implement antisemitic policies, whilst the situation in Palestine was becoming increasingly difficult.

A few Christians – alas, too few! – quickly recognised the need to combat antisemitism and to relieve the sufferings of the Jews. In 1934, for example, the General Assembly of the Church of Scotland, recognising the 'age-long sufferings of the Jewish people' and aware of 'the present outbreaks of anti-Semitic fanaticism', declared its heart-felt sympathy for the Jewish people and that their ill-treatment was 'abhorrent'.[11]

In 1934, a Youth Council on Jewish–Christian Relations was set up. This was initially a Christian initiative to alert young Christians to the dangers of antisemitism and to encourage friendly contact with young Jews. After a first meeting at Lincoln's Inn Fields, at which Dr Conrad Hoffmann spoke of a recent visit to Germany and described the 'cold pogrom' against Jews, it was agreed to approach other youth organisations. At the meeting it was hoped ways would be found of encouraging young people to visit the Continent and to discover what was happening. The importance of long-term re-education of Christians so that they had a proper understanding of Jews and Judaism was recognised. W.W. Simpson, whose name is frequently to recur in these pages, was asked to serve as secretary for the time being. Several Christian youth organisations agreed to join the council. At the time, it was decided not to invite Jewish organisations, although by 1940, it had developed into a joint Jewish–Christian youth organisation. Eventually the council was absorbed into CCJ.

The aims of the council, as set out in a paper presented to the International Committee on the Christian Approach to Jews, which met at Vienna in the summer of 1937, were educational and practical.

> The education of Christian Youth in a proper understanding of the Jewish people must be regarded as of fundamental importance. This must necessarily involve the study of Jewish history, life and religion, together with an impartial examination of the facts relating to the past and present relationships between the two Communities.

The practical programme included seeking friendly contacts between Jewish and Christian youth organisations, for the purpose of understanding, cooperation and real spiritual fellowship. It was clear that the council was not missionary in intention, which caused some questioning from other Christian organisations. The council produced a manual for group study, and arranged a series of meetings and a week-end 'Visit to Jewish London'.[12]

In the mid-1930s, refugees from Germany began to make their way to Britain. Various groups tried to offer help. There were several existing Jewish organisations, which found it increasingly difficult to cope with the flood of refugees. In 1936, an Inter-Aid Committee was formed, which was affiliated to the Save the Children Fund and which was under the chairmanship of Sir Wyndham Deedes. The committee included representatives of both Jewish and Christian caring agencies.

By late 1938, following Kristallnacht, the situation had deteriorated sharply. A Refugee Children's Movement was formed, upon the initiative of Mrs Norman Bentwich, with Viscount Samuel as chairman. The government agreed to admit greater numbers of children, on the basis of a 'travel-document' validated by the committee, instead of requiring visas. In March 1939, the committee was reconstituted with Lord Gorell as chairman. The committee received many offers of hospitality and did what it could to find suitable homes for the children. Care was taken to try to find Orthodox Jews to provide homes for children of Orthodox parents.

> Whenever a Jewish child was placed in a Christian home, it was laid down as a principle of the movement, and clearly understood by the host, that there was to be no proselytisation. Further, the child was put in touch with the nearest resident Rabbi, or religious instruction was arranged by correspondence.[13]

Following the Nuremburg Decrees, which held that anyone with a Jewish grandparent was Jewish, the number of 'non-Aryan' Christian refugees increased rapidly. In 1938, Anglican, Free Church and Roman Catholic Churches agreed to support a Christian Council for Refugees. The chairman was the leading Methodist, Rev. Henry Carter, well known for his work with the National Children's Homes, who was later to chair the Council of Christians and Jews for several years. Dr George Bell, the Bishop of Chichester, played a leading part in this organisation. The Rev. W. W. Simpson, who was to devote his life to improving Christian–Jewish relations, was appointed secretary.

W. W. SIMPSON

Bill Simpson was at that time a Methodist minister of Amhurst Park in North London, which was an area which included much of the Orthodox Hassidic Jewish community of Stamford Hill. He had, however, already become interested in Judaism at school and university. At school, he was conscious of Jewish boys who did not fit in. He was also entrusted with the Mandate for Palestine at an inter-school mock Assembly of the League of Nations. This made him do some study of the situation. In 1926, whilst a student at the Methodist theological college in Cambridge, he was invited to tea at another college by an undergraduate who insisted on coming to collect him. As they walked, his friend asked him whether he approved of Christians trying to convert Jews. He said he had not really thought about this. At tea, he met an Orthodox Jewish undergraduate. Simpson says he thinks his friend had perhaps been anxious lest he should try to influence the Jew. In fact, it was the other way round. Eventually Simpson was invited to the synagogue to hear the Chief Rabbi of Dublin, Dr Herzog, who was later to be the first Chief Rabbi of Israel.

After Cambridge, Simpson began to work on the fringe of the East End of London as a trainee Methodist minister. He had links with a Free Church missionary society and had seen from the inside something of the various Christian missions to the Jews. Increasingly he felt unhappy with this approach and was helped by a scholar whom he had met at Cambridge, Canon Lukyn Williams, who in his *Adversus Judaeos* had reacted strongly against traditional Christian efforts to persuade Jews of the errors of their ways. The authorities of the Methodist Church had also encouraged Simpson to devote two years to the study of contemporary Jewish problems. For that period he was a part-time student at Jews' College, a rabbinic seminary in London. He had also studied traditional Christian approaches to Jews.[14] He was, therefore, well prepared for his work for the Council for Refugees.

It is interesting that in a pamphlet called *The Christian and the Jewish Problem*, published by the Epworth Press in 1939, Simpson

1. Children of One God

2. Chief Rabbi Dr Hertz and Archbishop William Temple

3. HM The Queen, Patron of CCJ

was already looking beyond the immediate tragedy of the refugees and the horrors of Nazi persecution, to recognising the Christian share of responsibility for Jewish sufferings. 'It is important to realise', he writes, 'that one of the chief factors in forcing the Jews into a negative kind of separatism has been the attitude generally adopted by the Christian community.'[15] He mentions the charge of deicide, the attacks of the Crusaders, the institution of the Ghetto and the Inquisition. 'The underlying causes of the modern Jewish problem ... are to be found in that tragic combination of circumstances for which the past failure of the Christian community either to understand or to do justice to the Jews has been mainly responsible.'[16] The problem, he wrote, called for education. Christians needed a far better knowledge of Judaism. Too often they seemed to think, like Marcion, that the New Testament God was superior to the God of the Old Testament. Simpson recognised that modern Judaism was the creation of the Rabbis, who were the successors of the Pharisees. 'The history of the Jewish community in post-Biblical times is almost completely ignored in the modern educational syllabus.'[17]

Simpson stressed the need for Jewish–Christian cooperation, especially as the two religions faced a common enemy.

> In the past each has been guilty of injustice to the other, though it can hardly be disputed that the Christian has been the more to blame. To-day, however, these injustices, having been recognised by both parties, must be forgiven and forgotten as together they brace themselves to their supreme task of bearing witness, at whatever cost, in an increasingly hostile world, to the inviolability of the eternal qualities of righteousness, holiness, truth and justice, and of the redemptive principle of sacrificial suffering which for the Jew is enshrined in the Suffering Servant of the fifty-third chapter Isaiah and for the Christian in the life, death and resurrection of Jesus Christ.[18]

Simpson's life, as well as his words, were a witness to these eternal qualities.

2

The Beginnings

There are two accounts of the beginnings of the Council. One places these under a pear tree at Barley. James Parkes, in his auto-biography, says that it was there, in his own orchard, that he discussed the idea with Mrs Kathleen Freeman, a prominent Anglican lay-leader and one-time president of the National Council of Women. She then discussed it with Rabbi Mattuck of the Liberal Synagogue and with Bishop George Bell of Chichester. W.W. Simpson, however, claims that Bloomsbury House, where he was working at the Christian Council for Refugees, was the scene of the initial discussions. Certainly Mrs Freeman, who was a member of the Committee for Non-Aryan Christian Refugees, was a frequent visitor to Bloomsbury House.[1]

One suggestion was to build on the existing Society of Jews and Christians. A group originating from the Society met twice in 1941, under the leadership of The Dean of St Paul's, Very Rev. W. Matthews. Because of its 'great concern for the betterment of Jewish Christian relations, in view of certain perils to religion and civilization known to us all, the group had in view the formation of a Council with extensions in the country'.[2] The difficulty with this was that the Chief Rabbi, Dr J.H. Hertz, had often strongly criticized any form of 'religious fraternisation', which he regarded as 'neither desired nor desirable'. He had often cited the Society of Jews and Christians as a prime example of this. Yet, it was inconceivable that there should be any form of Council in which the Chief Rabbi did not take a leading part.

A LUNCH AT GROSVENOR HOUSE

An approach, therefore, was made by Rev. Henry Carter and others to William Temple, the Archbishop of York. He agreed to invite leaders of the communities to a lunch to discuss what should be done. Adolf Brotman, the Secretary of the Board of Deputies of British Jews, undertook to arrange a suitable meal for the Chief Rabbi. At the lunch held at Grosvenor House on 19 November 1941, the Chief Rabbi was provided with a basket of fresh fruit – a real luxury in war-time London – whilst Brotman himself had to make do with a hard-boiled egg. At the lunch, Temple and Hertz got on splendidly.

Temple was anxious to avoid specific mention of antisemitism. He saw it and the war itself as symptomatic of an even deeper evil and crisis. They were dealing, he said, 'with a problem of civilisation and not only the relationship between Jew and Christian'. The reaction to antisemitism had to be positive. Direct opposition

> both called attention to it and concentrated attention upon the division which they were trying to overcome … If they could find ways of expressing the principles which they had in common and which they agreed in thinking lay at the basis of a just civilisation, they would do very much more towards healing antisemitism than by any frontal attack. It was by the actual engagement of Jews and Christians together in the fuller understanding and operation of the principles which they had shaped together and which had their roots in the Old Testament scriptures that they could best deal with that which was rather a symptom than the essential disease.[3]

Temple here mapped out the path CCJ was to follow. It has set itself against all forms of discrimination and has tried to promote 'the fundamental ethical teachings which are common to Judaism and Christianity'. CCJ is not just a branch of Jewish defence nor a society of Christians for the protection of Jews, although outsiders have sometimes seen it in both guises. Its deepest task is to witness to the values which Jews and Christians hold in common and in which there is no place for prejudice, persecution or discrimination.

The Chief Rabbi affirmed this approach. The gathering, he said, had a unique opportunity to deal with

> a serious menace to the moral and spiritual life of Great Britain. The central point was … 'to consider the danger to civilisation involved in antisemitism, as well as the steps that might be taken by Christians, working in consultation with Jews to prevent its spread in this country'.

11

Antisemitism, he said, was a demon which could only be exorcised

by holy words spoken by holy men having authority. A
Church pronouncement like that of Pius XI in 1938 'Antisemitism is a movement in which we Christians can have no
part whatsoever. Spiritually we are Semites' had done and
could do, if repeated in the proper way, immeasurable good.

'National life and religion, civilisation', he continued, 'all depended
on the attitude of any society to the Jew.'

The Nazi creed, he said, was 'the deification of the state ... It was
the denial of mercy, justice, holiness; it was the utter repudiation of
the sacredness of human life.' CCJ, as the Chief Rabbi recognised
at the beginning, is concerned, at its heart, to preserve human
dignity and decency and to defend biblical morality. Antisemitism
symbolises the continuing threat to civilisation and religion.

Dr Hertz referred to the putting to death of the mentally ill, with
the approval of the German government. He also complained that
the press was callous in its reports of Jewish suffering under the
Nazis and underestimated the number of Jewish deaths.

Hertz was very clear that each community must be responsible
for its own religious teaching. He wanted to avoid any suggestion
that Jews should get to know about Christian teaching. 'There
should not be interference with Jewish teaching, and the least
suspicion that Jews were in any way interfering with the religious
teaching in Christian schools was unthinkable and could not be
contemplated.' This was a matter which was to cause further difficulty. He once again distanced himself from 'religious fraternisation'.[4]

Rev. Henry Carter spoke about the document which had been
circulated prior to the meeting. I have not discovered a surviving
copy of this document, but from what Henry Carter said some idea
of its contents can be reconstructed. The document outlined the
possible work of a council. Paragraph One referred to difficulties
caused by evacuation and the provision of air-raid shelters. Local
problems might foment antisemitism and required a twofold witness against it. Paragraph Two spoke of cooperation between youth
organisations, but this caused some fear that it could lead to 'an
invasion of the convictions of either group'. Paragraph Three, in its
first part, spoke of 'the effective checking or combatting of antisemitism through literature, the press and the spoken word'. The

second part mentioned checking antisocial teachings in either community, but this was a matter on which the Chief Rabbi had hesitations as it could seem like 'interference'. Paragraph Four suggested that Jews and Christians together needed to defend their shared ethical tradition and the values of civilisation.[5]

Bishop Mathew, who was representing Cardinal Hinsley, stressed that for Catholics it was the religious link with Jews that was uppermost. He shared the Chief Rabbi's hesitations about any suggestion that outsiders should advise a community about the religious teaching which it gave to its young. Dr Mattuck, of the Liberal Jewish tradition, stressed the need for all sections of the Jewish community and for all Churches to be involved in the work.

On Sir Robert Waley Cohen's proposal, seconded by Dr Daiches of Edinburgh, it was agreed 'that a committee be appointed to prepare a basis of and constitution for a council to carry forward the work of the conference as outlined in the invitation, with due regard to what has been said in the conference'. After Rabbi Untermann, who was Communal Rabbi of Liverpool, and the Chief Rabbi had again made clear that no interference with the religious teaching of any community was envisaged, the resolution was carried unanimously. It was agreed that the Archbishop should, in consultation, choose the seven Christian representatives on the committee and that the Chief Rabbi and Professor Brodetsky should choose the seven Jews. Mr Simpson and Mr Brotman were asked to act as convenors.

AGREEMENT TO FORM CCJ

It was on 20 March 1942 that the decision was taken to form the Council of Christians and Jews. At that meeting, chaired by William Temple, whose nomination to be Archbishop of Canterbury had just been announced, the report of the continuation group, which had met on 8 January 1942, was accepted.

The formal resolution reads:

> That this Conference of representatives of the Christian and Jewish communities in Great Britain constitutes itself as The Council of Christians and Jews. The Council shall have power of co-option up to a maximum membership of 50.

The agreed aims of the Council were:

13

That since the Nazi attack on Jewry has revealed that anti-semitism is part of a general and comprehensive attack on Christianity and Judaism and on the ethical principles common to both religions which form the basis of the free national life of Great Britain the Council adopts the following aims:

(a) To check and combat religious and racial intolerance.

(b) To promote mutual understanding and goodwill between Christians and Jews in all sections of the community, especially in connection with problems arising from conditions created by the war.

(c) To promote fellowship between Christian and Jewish youth organisations in educational and cultural activities.

(d) To foster co-operation of Christians and Jews in study and service directed to post-war reconstruction.

It was agreed to invite the Archbishop of Canterbury, the Moderator of the Church of Scotland, the Moderator of the Free Church Federal Council and the Chief Rabbi to be joint presidents. William Temple accepted on the spot. Bishop Mathew explained that Cardinal Hinsley would not feel able to accept such an invitation, although he wished to do all he could to check antisemitism and racism. An Executive Committee was set up, with a maximum membership of 20. Its Christian members were Very Rev. W. Matthews, Rev. Henry Carter, Rev. James Fraser, Mr W. Littleboy, Rev. Dr James Parkes, Rev. S. Berry and Mr A. C. F. Beales. The Jewish members were Professor S. Brodetsky, Sir Robert Waley Cohen, Mr Leonard J. Stein, Dr I. I. Mattuck, Dr I. Feldman and Mr Anthony de Rothschild. Mr Brotman and Rev. W. W. Simpson were appointed joint secretaries.

It was agreed that expenses should be met 'on the basis of contributions equal as far as practicable from the Christian and Jewish communities'. In fact, the bulk of the money of the Council was to come from Jewish sources. For a few years the Board of Deputies gave a generous annual contribution. It may be that had the religious communities themselves taken on the financing rather than leaving this to the generosity of individuals the work of the Council would have been on a firmer foundation.[6]

It is worth making clear that initially CCJ was a small self-perpetuating oligarchic body. Initially membership was limited to 50, although quite soon this figure was increased to 200. At Dr

Parkes' suggestion, an associate membership of sympathetic individuals was created, but they had no say in the running of the Council. It was not until the 1980s that the structure was changed and the Council became a democratic body in which members of the Executive were elected by members.

There was also an ambiguity in the relationship of the Council to the religious communities. The initiative to form a Council received – indeed it required – the backing of the highest religious leaders. It was not clear to what extent it was subject to their control and to what extent it was an independent body. This ambiguity was to cause various difficulties in the future.

THE FIRST EXECUTIVE MEETING

No time was wasted. The first meeting of the Executive followed immediately after the inaugural meeting. The contentious issue of the relation of the Council to 'conversionist bodies' was raised almost at once. Mr Carter asked whether the Council should be prepared to accept financial contributions 'from individuals or organisations connected with or engaged in conversionist activities'. It was agreed that 'the Council was a body through which neither conversionist activities or hopes would be promoted' and that this must be observed in connection with the raising of funds.

At the following meeting, on 13 April 1942, Dr Temple was asked to serve as chairman of the Executive. Although in fact Henry Carter, as vice-chairman, usually took the chair at Executive meetings, Temple agreed and he always chaired Council meetings. There is considerable evidence of his close personal attention to the affairs of the Council. It is surprising, therefore, that there is no reference to CCJ in the index of F.A. Iremonger's biography of William Temple.

THE CHIEF RABBI'S THREAT TO WITHDRAW

During the summer of 1942 preparations continued to be made for a public announcement of the Council's formation and a constitution was prepared. In June, however, the whole fragile and elaborate structure nearly collapsed. Dr Hertz, the Chief Rabbi, wrote to Archbishop Temple informing him that he felt in duty bound to dissociate orthodox Jewry and himself from membership of the Executive Committee. His reasons were twofold. He had made clear from the beginning that there could be no Jewish interference in Christian teaching or vice versa. He felt that the 'Projects in the Educational Field' accepted by the Executive on 4 June conflicted with this position. He also complained that Orthodox Jews were not adequately represented on the Executive, especially as he himself, because of ill health, had been unable to attend meetings. In response to this latter point, the Executive, in suggesting the reply that the Archbishop might make, said that the nomination of Jewish members had been left to the Jewish community and that earlier in the meeting it had been agreed to invite Dr A. Cohen of Birmingham to join the Executive. With regard to the possibility of preparing pamphlets for Christian readers about the Pharisees and about Jewish life and Jewish festivals, it was understood that this was a matter for the Christian members of the Executive and not an activity of the Council *per se*.

At the following Executive on 8 July, the Archbishop, who was in the chair, said he had talked with the Chief Rabbi. The Chief Rabbi had asked for the appointment of Dayan Lazarus and Rabbi Unterman to the Executive. After consultation with the Jewish members of the Executive, this was agreed. On the educational projects, the offending minute was replaced by these words:

'Projects in the Educational Field'

(a) The importance of securing a fair presentation in elementary, secondary and Sunday School education of the position of the Jews.

The Executive, while recognising the importance of this matter, regarded it as lying beyond its scope; it was agreed to ask the Christian members of the Executive to seek ways of using their personal influence in the matter apart from the Council.[7]

Dr Hertz had also suggested that a copy of the letter to him, in which the Archbishop set out the principles of cooperation on which he conceived the Council to be established, be sent to all members of the Council.

Part of that letter, of 2 July 1942, was eventually to be included in the constitution of the Council, and deserves to be quoted:

My own approach to this matter is governed by the consideration that the effectiveness of any religious belief depends upon its definiteness, and that neither Jews nor Christians should in my judgment combine in any such way as to obscure the distinctiveness of their witness to their own beliefs. There is much that we can do together in combating religious and racial intolerance, in forwarding social progress and in bearing witness to those moral principles which we unite in upholding.[8]

CARDINAL HINSLEY

Having resolved the difficulties with the Chief Rabbi, the Executive was encouraged by news that Cardinal Hinsley was willing to become a Joint President. There were two conditions. One was that any statement to be signed by the Joint Presidents or to go out from the Executive should be submitted to him well in advance. The other was that he should be represented on the Executive by Bishop Mathew, who was Secretary of the Catholic organisation the Sword of the Spirit.[9]

With Cardinal Hinsley's decision, the complement of joint presidents was complete – at least, until 1988. In that year, the leader of the Greek Orthodox Community, the Archbishop of Thyateira and Great Britain, became a joint president. Suggestions that the Reform or Liberal Jewish communities should have a joint president have always been resisted on the grounds that the Chief Rabbi, who is the leader of the Orthodox Jewish community, claims to speak on public matters and in relationship to the Churches for the whole Jewish community.

The newly formed body was therefore assured of official approval and backing, although it has remained a voluntary organisation, answerable for some years to a Council and now to the Executive, which is elected by the members.

PUBLIC ANNOUNCEMENT

All was now set for the public announcement of the Council's formation, which was made in *The Times* 'and other organs of the Press' on 1 October 1942 and reported the previous evening on the BBC's nine o'clock news.

The statement is of lasting interest:

The following Statement is issued by the Archbishop of Canterbury, the Moderator of the General Assembly of the Church of Scotland, the Moderator of the Free Church Federal Council, and the Chief Rabbi of the United Hebrew Congregations of the British Empire:

The present German Government has consistently attempted to undermine and destroy those traditional religious and spiritual values of mankind in which it recognises its most dangerous enemies. The course of the war has seen a steady intensification of these attempts, and German conquests have enormously extended the area in which these policies can be ruthlessly applied.

In the forefront of their efforts to create division within every community the Nazis have always placed anti-semitism, which is repugnant to the moral principles common to Christianity and Judaism alike. We cannot afford to ignore the effects of the steady propagation of this evil throughout the world. It is not only a menace to the unity of every community in which it takes root, but it is the very negation of those values on which alone we believe that a new and better world can be established.

In these circumstances we are agreed that it would be for the general benefit to form in this country a Council of Christians and Jews, which might draw to itself the support in this matter of all men and women of goodwill. Such a Council has now been formed and, as Joint Presidents, we have been gratified by the influential and whole-hearted response which has been immediately forthcoming.

The aims of the Council are:

(a) To check and combat religious and racial intolerance.
(b) To promote mutual understanding and goodwill between Christians and Jews in all sections of the community, especially in connection with problems arising from conditions created by the war.
(c) To promote fellowship between Christian and Jewish youth organisations in educational and cultural activities.

(d) To foster cooperation of Christians and Jews in study and service directed to post-war reconstruction . . .

His Eminence Cardinal Hinsley, Archbishop of Westminster, endorses the condemnation of antisemitism and has, since the composition of this statement, joined the Council as a Joint President as a mark of his strong protest against all persecution of the Jewish people.[10]

In an editorial, the *Jewish Chronicle* hailed the news as 'A Great Step Forward'.

We have a formal and authoritative recognition that anti-semitism is not a matter for Jews alone, but a challenge of equal if not greater gravity to non-Jews. It is *their* national unity, *their* moral and religious status, *their* dearest hopes for the future, which the assault on Jews and Judaism is placing in direct jeopardy. It is certainly a Christian quite as much as a Jewish peril. That is what the formation of this Council means.

In a prophetic paragraph the editorial warns against expecting quick results.

The public must be on its guard against impatient clamour for concrete results of the Council's endeavour. Some may, indeed, evidence themselves here and there. But the full effects of the quiet and patient labours now to begin will not be measurable or ponderable at any given hour of any given day. Indeed, it may well turn out that the greater the blessings which labours of the Council bestow, the less obvious or even noticeable their results may be immediately to the public eye. Deep-seated evils cannot be eradicated by the waving of a magic wand. The powers of wickedness, ignorance and thoughtlessness, of long-inherited prejudice, cannot easily be conjured away. The Kingdom of God is not to be handed to restless spirits on a platter. Much care and devotion must go to its building, and perhaps many setbacks, disappointments, and heart-breaks.[11]

3

The Early Years

THE NAZI HORROR

The Council of Christians and Jews was formed in the shadow of the Nazi menace. Even so, the references in the minutes to Nazi horrors are not perhaps as frequent as might have been expected. It is easy 50 years later to forget both the difficulty, in war-time, of acquiring exact information and sheer incredulity that such atrocities were possible. Even now, it is not possible to comprehend the terror of the Shoah. It is beyond both our understanding and imagination.

At the Executive meeting on 3 December 1942, Rev. Henry Carter, who was in the chair, voiced his sense of horror and moral indignation at the 'news recently to hand of the ruthless pursuit of a policy of extermination of European Jewry by the Nazi authorities'.[1] Jewish members expressed appreciation of the courageous opposition of some continental Christian leaders to the Nazis. Possible lines of action were suggested. It was decided that a deputation should approach the Foreign Office to discover the authenticity of reports of what was happening to Jews in Eastern Europe. It was also agreed that church leaders needed to inform the minds and consciences of Christian people about what was happening, although some expressed concern lest the public was already sated with 'horror stories'. There was also a suggestion that leaders of the Churches should raise the question of a Declaration of the United Nations and in particular see what could be done to help Jews escape – many countries still had strict controls on the entry of refugees to their lands and entry to Palestine was also strictly controlled by the British Mandatory authorities.

The following Monday, the Executive met again. By that time, Carter had had three telephone conversations with Temple. Temple had undertaken to ask for a meeting with Mr Eden during the coming week. He had also written to *The Times*, following its article on Friday 4 December about the fate of Jews in Eastern Europe. In his letter, which appeared on 5 December, he spoke of a 'horror beyond what imagination can grasp'. Speaking for Free Church friends as well as for the Church of England he expressed 'our burning indignation at this atrocity, to which the records of barbarous ages scarcely supply a parallel'. He recognised the difficulty of knowing what to do. 'At least we might offer to receive here any Jews who are able to escape the clutches of the Nazis and make their way to our shores.' He criticised the delays of officialdom. 'In comparison with the monstrous evil confronting us the reasons for hesitation usually advanced by officials have an air of irrelevance.' He also suggested the possible prosecution after the war of those held responsible. I have not been able to discover if others had already mentioned the idea of war crimes trials. 'It could be announced that any person proved to be directly or indirectly concerned in this outrage would be held responsible when the war is over.'[2] The Executive again mentioned a wish to see the United Nations jointly express their condemnation and again urged the Foreign Office to open possible ways of escape.

The deputation, which consisted only of Christian members of the Executive, met Mr Richard Law, Under-Secretary of State for the Foreign Office, on 16 December. No specific promise had been made to make it easier for refugees to escape and it was agreed to ask the Archbishop to take this up with the Prime Minister. On 3 February 1943, the Colonial Secretary agreed to the admission of some Jewish children, with a proportion of adults, to Palestine. The following day, the first annual meeting of the Council was held. At this, a resolution was passed welcoming government promises to do more to help refugees who escaped to countries beyond German control. It was suggested that the British government might give temporary asylum in British territories, including Palestine, to anyone who escaped. Together with the United Nations, assurances should be given to neutral countries that help would be available to cope with refugees. The Government was also urged to warn the perpetrators of the consequences.[3]

At subsequent meetings considerable attention was given to helping refugees and the bodies involved in this work. The Council repeatedly expressed its horror at Nazi atrocities and called on the

British people to repudiate all forms of antisemitism. In November 1943, for example, the Council reasserted 'its belief in the sacredness of human life and in the equality of all men before God, principles which are common to both Judaism and Christianity, and utterly condemns the denial to any section of mankind of their fundamental rights'.[4] Early the following year, news reached Britain of the worsening plight of Jews in Central Europe, especially with the Nazi takeover in Hungary. The Archbishop, at the Council's suggestion, broadcast on the BBC World Service to the people of Hungary. He appealed to Christians there

> to do your utmost to save from persecution, it may be from massacre, those who are now threatened as a result of German occupation ... Help them to hide from their tormentors, help them, if possible, to escape. Do all you can to prevent the extermination of people whose only fault is the race from which they are born or the independence of their minds and constancy of their convictions.[5]

Temple felt deeply his powerlessness to bring effective help to the millions who he knew were being starved, tortured and murdered. He had to balance the effectiveness of private appeal and protest to the government against public statements which might put ministers on the defensive. Ministers asked the Archbishop to consider that displaced persons might be members, in disguise, of a Nazi or Communist cell. They also asked him to consider the possibility of an outbreak of antisemitism in Britain, if special favour was shown to Jews. (Some newspapers delighted to publish the names of those Jews who were guilty of black market offences.) It was also suggested that Hitler might find excuse for further barbarities if he could say that the Jews were now seen to be friends of Britain and therefore the enemies of the Fatherland.[6]

By early 1943, it was clear nothing said in Britain could worsen the plight of Jews who were under Nazi control. On 23 March, therefore, Temple moved in the House of Lords:

> That, in view of the massacres and starvation of Jews and others in enemy and enemy-occupied countries, this House desires to assure His Majesty's Government of its fullest support for immediate measures, on the largest and most generous scale compatible with the requirements of military

operations and security, for providing help and temporary asylum to persons in danger of massacre who are able to leave enemy and enemy-occupied countries.[7]

Temple quoted figures of the massacres, made several suggestions and asked that a person of high standing in the government or civil service should be appointed to make this his first concern. He protested strongly against the government's procrastination. He admitted that what anyone could do was small,

> but we cannot rest so long as there is any sense among us that we are not doing all that might be done. We have discussed the matter on the footing that we are not responsible for this great evil, that the burden lies on others, but it is always true that the obligations of decent men are decided for them by contingencies which they did not themselves create and very largely by the action of wicked men ... We at this moment have upon us a tremendous responsibility. We stand at the bar of history, of humanity, and of God.[8]

With news of the Buchenwald massacres in 1944, he again spoke out. He remained convinced that, whether or not a word from him would be effective at any given moment, 'it ought to be said for the sake of the principles of justice itself, and I shall continue the advocacy which I have endeavoured to offer hitherto'.[9] This is not the place to discuss government action, which Temple found desperately slow and prevaricating. It is, however, important to recognise that from the beginning Temple vigorously opposed Nazi actions, which he saw as a direct threat to the values of Judaism and Christianity. He spoke persistently in defence of the Jews. Much is said of the silence of the Churches, which was often all too evident: but Temple, with the support of leaders of all Churches, was outspoken on the issue. He was only too well aware how little was achieved, but all of us are aware of how difficult it is to oppose ruthless evil. Temple at least saw the evil for the hideous bestiality that it was and did not ignore it himself nor allow others to divert their gaze. His death was deeply mourned in the Jewish community, as elsewhere. The World Jewish Congress spoke of him as the champion of the Jews. 'His interest in Jews was not a by-product of his sacred duties ... Profoundly conscious of the physical suffering of the Jews, and acutely sensitive to its spiritual significance, he was at all times ready to make every contribution to the alleviation of the great tragedy that had befallen a great people.'[10]

After the war the Council's concern with the plight of displaced persons was unabated. This was voiced at the 1946 annual meeting. The following year an Executive meeting, held on 10 September 1947, at the suggestion of its Christian members, passed a strong resolution expressing 'profound dismay' about the fate of 4,500 Jewish refugees who, on board the *Exodus*, had tried illegally to enter Palestine. The ship had been intercepted by the British. Not only were the refugees not allowed to land, they were not even allowed to disembark in Cyprus. In fact, they were taken back to the displaced persons camps in Germany – the land of the Holocaust – from which they had set out. There was international condemnation of this action and CCJ made its views clear. 'The Committee does not believe that if the Government could not allow them to land in Palestine, it was impossible to detain them in Cyprus or some other place within British control less charged with bitter memories than the soil of Germany.'[11]

PALESTINE/ISRAEL

Soon after the war, national attention focused on the political situation in Palestine. The violence of extreme Jewish groups there was quickly condemned by leaders of the Jewish community in Britain, as well as by Christian leaders. The Council condemned these acts, which were 'a fundamental violation of the spiritual and ethical principles common to Judaism and Christianity'. The Council warned against 'any tendency to condemn Jews as a whole for the crimes of a numerically insignificant minority'.[12]

The Council's concern, properly, was with the effect that events in Palestine were having on Jewish–Christian relations in Britain. Its remit was not with the political situation in Palestine *per se*. The Executive, in May 1946, when reference was made to the Report of the Anglo-American Committee of Enquiry Regarding the Problems of European Jewry and Palestine, recognised that this matter lay outside its competence. Again, when the terrorist outrages were first discussed at the Executive, it was again recognised that CCJ was not competent to pronounce on the political situation.[13]

With the creation of the state of Israel, Christian anxiety was expressed about the fate of the refugees and about the safety and sanctity of the holy places in Jerusalem.

Archbishop Fisher took a deep personal interest in the situation in Palestine. He received many letters, often from correspondents who sharply disagreed with each other. Fisher was strongly opposed to antisemitism, which, he wrote, 'was not a matter of being pro-Jewish, but of fighting racial prejudice and passion where it exists'. He was concerned for Jewish refugees and took up with Oliver Stanley, the Secretary of State for the Colonies, the plight of 1500 Jewish refugees who had been shipped off to Mauritius. Fisher did, however, oppose extreme statements of the Jewish case. With reluctance, he came to feel that a federal solution or partition was necessary.

Fisher was a strong advocate of international control of Jerusalem, which was also advocated by the Pope. Indeed he took the unprecedented step of putting forward his own plan, under the aegis of the World Council of Churches, which he submitted to the United Nations in December 1949. Fisher suggested an international *enclave* in the heart of Jerusalem in which Jew and Arab would have equal rights. There would be one administrative authority under the trusteeship of the United Nations. He had a vision of Jerusalem as a spiritual and global centre where Jews and Arabs could together 'ennoble the spirit of mankind'. The suggestion, which was his own and not made on behalf of CCJ, gained little support and caused the government some embarrassment. It seems that Fisher came to wonder whether his intervention had been wise, but comforted himself with the thought that it had not 'made a bad situation worse'.[14]

In his address to the annual meeting on 23 November 1949, the Chief Rabbi, Dr Israel Brodie, took up the question of Israel. He said that the establishment of the state had had 'a tremendous effect on Jews throughout the world'. He recognised that many Christians had fears and concerns about the safeguarding of and free access to the Holy Places. He also acknowledged Christian concern about the plight of Arab refugees. He asked the Council to continue to express goodwill towards the new state and to regard it with charity and to remember it in prayer. He admitted that mistakes had been and would be made. 'It will', he said, 'in that regard be no different from any other Government' – although Christians have often measured Israel's behaviour against their exaggerated expectations. He pointed to the extreme difficulties which Israel was facing.[15]

ANTI-JEWISH FEELING IN BRITAIN

One cause of anti-Jewish feeling in Britain was the accusation that many Jews were involved in the 'black market'. The matter was broached at the fourth meeting of the Executive. Efforts were made to obtain accurate statistical information. Meetings were arranged with government ministers. A deputation from the Council met with Sir Stephen Low, Solicitor to the Board of Trade. It seems that many of the early prosecutions were in the clothes trade, in which a large number of Jews were engaged. It became clear that, proportionately, no more Jews were guilty of offences than other members of the population.

Complaint was made about the tone of some religious films being shown to the troops, which were negative in their view of Judaism.

Another issue that was soon raised and which has recurred periodically, was that of *Shechita* – the Jewish method of slaughtering animals for food. In 1943, Leeds Branch of the Royal Society for the Prevention of Cruelty to Animals raised questions about this method of slaughter. Similar questions have been raised quite regularly by animal welfare groups. CCJ has maintained that *Shechita* is at least as humane as other legal methods of animal slaughter. It has also been aware that this is an emotional subject sometimes used by those who are antisemitic.[16]

At the May 1943 meeting of the Executive, Sir Wyndham Deedes introduced a discussion of antisemitism that he felt was 'alarmingly on the increase', particularly amongst the 'so-called better educated classes'. He thought that to publicise more facts about the number of Jews serving in the armed forces might help.[17]

It was suggested that an approach might be made to the BBC to broadcast some talks about Jews and Judaism. At the time, they had a strict policy of only referring to Judaism in specifically religious programmes. Whilst the Council was always vigilant about any signs of antisemitism, in general, there was a reluctance directly to confront it, lest this made matters worse. It has always been difficult to decide when public statements and protests are helpful and when they may trigger 'copy-cat' action. Early on, the Council made clear that its primary task was a long-term educational one.

At the first meeting of local councils, held in 1947, the Marquess of Reading, who was in the chair, explained that the Council had never been primarily concerned to do open battle with the cruder forms of antisemitism, but hoped 'by promoting intimate and informed understanding between Christians and Jews upon the fundamental aspects of life to create a solid basis of harmony founded upon a recognition of similarities and a respect for differences'.[18]

EDUCATIONAL WORK

From the beginning, CCJ set a high priority on educational work, which would help Jews and Christians come to a proper appreciation of each other's faith and which would help remove distorting stereotypes and prejudices.

In 1949, Albert Polack was appointed Education Officer. Albert had been born and brought up in Bristol. He was educated at Clifton College where his father, Rev. Joseph Polack, was the first housemaster of Polack's House. Albert himself became housemaster in 1926. When he 'retired' in 1949, he took on the very active job of Education Officer for CCJ. He stayed in this position until 1968. He then retired again and moved back to Bristol, where he continued his interest in both CCJ and the World Congress of Faiths, until his death, at the age of ninety, in 1982.

Besides the talks to schools and other audiences given by Polack and the rest of the staff, the Council pursued its educational policy through its publications. In 1943, the first issue of the bulletin, which became known as *Common Ground*, appeared. It is said that the bold red title was designed by Simpson himself, who borrowed some lipstick from one of the secretaries. Copies were sent to members and to colleges and schools. Initially copies were also taken by W.H. Smith's and Wyman's.

Common Ground gave information about the two faiths and news of the developing relationship between them. 'Each issue', the first edition proclaimed,

> will contain two or three short articles on matters of mutual interest and concern to Christians and Jews, though they may not deal specifically with relations between the two communities. There will be a series of jottings from the Secretary's

27

notebook, and news items about the work of local Councils and Societies of Jews and Christians in other countries ... Information about current literature and pamphlets will constitute another feature and a correspondence column is another possibility.[19]

By the early 1950s a circulation of about 2,500 had been reached.

Pamphlets were also produced. One of the first was entitled *Tolerance – Can It Be Taught* by Albert Polack. In 1955, after a survey of history textbooks used by the 11–15 age group, a booklet called *History Without Bias* appeared. In the 1950s, too, the Waley Cohen lecture was published regularly.

Another educational activity was in universities, in conjunction with denominational student societies. Local councils were also active in educational work. In East London, CCJ was working with the Council of Citizens of East London. Together four film strips were produced on 'One God: The Ways He is Worshipped and Served'. Increasingly CCJ found itself helping other organisations which wanted to give some attention to Christian–Jewish relations.

The Committee also set up special study groups on the issue of Religious Liberty and on the problems of the Near East.[19]

POST-WAR RECONSTRUCTION

From the beginning it was felt that Jews and Christians had much to contribute together to post war reconstruction. Early in the war, attention focused on 'Ten Points'. Five of these were proposals for the peace made by the Pope and five were economic standards agreed at the Oxford Conference of the Churches. They were used as a basis for 'Religion and Life' meetings, arranged by the Churches. At the second meeting of the Executive, it was agreed to see whether Jewish leaders could support the 'Ten Points'. Initially Dayan Lazarus voiced some concern that this could lead to 'religious indifferentism'.

Attention also focused on 'The Declaration of the United Nations'. The term United Nations, which now is normally used of the organisation set up after the war, was used at the time by the nations opposed to the so-called Axis powers – Germany, Italy and Japan. On 1 January 1942, 26 states signed 'The Declaration of the United Nations', in which were set out the war aims of the Allied powers. From time to time the suggestion was made that the United Nations should add to these aims, by promising help to people and countries who assisted refugees in escaping from Nazi regimes.

CCJ also supported the 'Three Faith Declaration' on post-war reconstruction drawn up in the USA and signed by many leading Protestants, Catholics and Jews.[20] In a statement agreed by the Executive, the Council affirmed that 'there can be no permanent peace without a religious foundation'. All social righteousness had to rest on divine law. 'The re-establishment of moral law, of respect for the rights of the person, especially those of the poor, the weak and the backward, and of responsibility towards the whole community, must be the first charges on the energies of all right-thinking men and women.'[21]

After the war, Canon Raven, Regius Professor at Cambridge, suggested that the Council might be a model of how people of all faiths might get together and discuss their common problems. 'Unless that can be done', he said, 'representatives of the United Nations can hardly take religion into its programme, for the United Nations embraces supporters of the five great faiths and of many others.'[22]

INTERNATIONAL AND LOCAL LINKS

Considerable effort was devoted in the early years of CCJ to building up both international and local links. We shall return to these developments in special chapters. Passing mention needs to be made of the Oxford Conference, which although international in character had a particular impact in Britain, especially because on the eve of the conference a crowded public meeting was held in London.[23]

THE LONDON SOCIETY OF JEWS AND CHRISTIANS

The Society of Jews and Christians was already well established before the formation of CCJ. It should not be considered a local council, although the suggestion was made that it might become a London Council of Christians and Jews, as almost all its members were in the London area. After some discussion, however, it was agreed that a functional differentiation would be more acceptable. The Society, renamed the London Society of Jews and Christians, 'would continue as hitherto to organise lectures and conferences in the London area and to publish occasional papers'. The Society has continued to maintain a high intellectual level and has not been constrained to avoid theological discussions.[24]

SCOTLAND

Early in 1943, on 27 January, a conference – the first of its kind – was held in Scotland, at the invitation of the Church of Scotland and attended by representatives of other Scottish Churches and of the Glasgow and Edinburgh Jewish communities. Support was expressed for the resolution of representatives of the Presbyterian Churches of Great Britain and Ireland, adopted a year before, in which all discrimination against Jews had been condemned. A continuation committee was also established.

ADMINISTRATIVE DEVELOPMENTS

The Council began its life in offices at Bloomsbury House, where the Christian Council for Refugees was housed, for which Simpson was working. By the end of 1942, an approach was made to release Simpson from his position at the Council so that he could become full-time organising secretary for CCJ. The Council for Refugees agreed, although it asked that Simpson might remain as administrative officer of Bloomsbury House, which he did until the autumn of 1945. Simpson, whose work was already widely appreciated, could now devote his full energies to CCJ. His salary at the time was £750 per annum. The assistant secretary was Mr George Lee. The office also seems to have been well provided with secretarial help.[25] In 1947, the Council had to leave Bloomsbury House and moved to rather cramped accommodation in the Strand.

Work quickly began on preparing a constitution for the Council, but this became a very protracted matter. The difficulty was the refusal for a long time of the Charity Commissioners and Income Tax officials to accept CCJ as a charity. Even a personal appeal by the joint presidents to the Chancellor of the Exchequer was ineffectual. Eventually, a constitution was adopted at an Extraordinary Meeting held on 20 February 1946. Legal advice was that the question of charitable status could only be resolved by appeal against a refusal to grant tax exemption to an actual payment under covenant to the Council. Before that could happen, a constitution had to be adopted. The constitution referred back to the aims agreed in March 1942 and to Archbishop Temple's letter to the Chief Rabbi, which has been quoted above.[26] Eventually, in 1948, the Council's status as a charity was recognised, although in 1964 the Council had to be reconstituted with a new constitution to satisfy changes in the charity laws.

The delay in granting charitable status impeded attempts to raise money, which then, as always, has been a problem. It was hoped that some money might come from the introduction of associate membership. This was open to members of local councils and other individuals who supported the Council's aims. The scheme was not as lucrative as had been hoped. Indeed, in 1947 the financial situation was so acute that there was talk about the possibility of winding up the Council.

In 1951, Henry Carter, who had been chairman of the Executive almost from the beginning, died. Many tributes were paid to his work. Speaking some years later, Archbishop Fisher said, 'The Council will never forget the great power that radiated from Henry Carter – the power of spirit, and of intelligence, and understanding and enthusiasm'.[27] Carter was succeeded by Professor Charles Raven, who chaired the executive until 1958.

The year after Carter's death, Sir Robert Waley Cohen, who had been active from the beginning, and who was the treasurer, also died. Robert Waley Cohen, head of a large industrial enterprise, had also been president of the United Synagogue and a vice-chairman of University College, London. His abiding concern was toleration. The Waley Cohen Lectures were founded in his memory and, appropriately, the first, given by Sir Richard Livingstone, was on 'Tolerance in Theory and in Practice'. Sir Robert Waley Cohen was succeeded as treasurer by Mr Edmund de Rothschild.

CONCLUSION

By 1952, despite the deaths of several pioneers, the Council was ten years old. It was well established and had received the patronage of the new Queen. The state of Israel, although the boundaries were still insecure, was established and had offered a home to many Jews who survived the Nazi holocaust. In Britain, Labour had been replaced by a Conservative government and gradually the post-war restrictions and rationing began to disappear. The growing prosperity eased some tensions in society. Whilst ever vigilant for signs of renewed antisemitism, CCJ was increasingly giving attention to longer-term educational work. Early hopes of formal international links had been disappointed, although informal contacts continued. CCJ showed its opposition to racism, especially in South Africa, as well as to all forms of discrimination, by voicing its concern about denials of religious freedom in Eastern Europe. Indeed the threat to religious life in the Communist bloc was seen by some as an added reason for Christian–Jewish cooperation in defence of a religious view of life.[28]

4

Catholic Withdrawal and Return

CATHOLIC WITHDRAWAL

In November 1954, a heavy blow fell on the Council. Cardinal Griffin intimated that he would be withdrawing from the joint presidency of CCJ on instructions from Rome. By a strange coincidence, I started writing this chapter on 2 November 1990, exactly 36 years to the day from W. W. Simpson's visit to Archbishop's House, Westminster, to be told by Msgr Warlock of the Cardinal's decision.

Immediately other resignations followed. Lord Perth resigned as joint honorary treasurer, and from the Council, and he was followed by other leading Roman Catholics. All expressed their deep regret at this move and their continuing sympathy with the work of the Council. As Canon Fitzgerald said, 'We here have got on like a house on fire ... I shall still feel the same about your work – I don't tolerate Jews; I like 'em'.[1]

In his formal letter of resignation, Cardinal Griffin wrote that CCJ

> appears now to be pursuing a policy which strictly was not envisaged at the time of the formation of the Council in 1942 nor when I succeeded Cardinal Hinsley as Joint President nearly eleven years ago. Whereas in those days the main emphasis of the Council's work lay on countering anti-semitism and on cooperation between Christians and Jews in regard to problems arising principally from conditions created by the war, the emphasis seems now to have shifted to the educational field where the promotion of mutual understanding is being conducted in a way likely to produce religious indifferentism.

The Cardinal went on to reaffirm his 'sympathy with and willing-

33

ness to help in any sincere attempt to defend the rights of the human person, whether it be a question of antisemitism or of any other person suffering persecution and violence'.[2]

At this difficult moment, the Archbishop of Canterbury, Dr Fisher, was very supportive. 'I am sure', he wrote, 'we ought not to be in any sense craven-hearted over this very disappointing action. It is indeed profoundly distressing, but I am sure the thing we must not accept is that Christian cooperation, and the degrees of it, should always be reconciled to the particular demands of the Church of Rome'.[3] Others who gave strong support were Canon Raven, Regius Professor at Cambridge who was chairman of the Executive, Rev. E. Benson Perkins, the Moderator of the Free Church Federal Council, the Chief Rabbi and Dr Jarvis, the Moderator of the General Assembly of the Church of Scotland. All helped draft the Council's reply which, whilst expressing regret at the Cardinal's decision, rejected any suggestion that the Council had departed 'either in principle or in practice' from the sincere pursuit of its original objectives.

In a reply, the Cardinal said that the Vatican was fully informed about CCJ. He then spelt out Catholic objections. These were not to the objects of the Council, but to aspects of its educational programme that involved not merely social and also moral matters but questions of faith. In particular there was objection to 'trio teams', in which a Catholic, a Protestant and a Jew discussed such matters. Several articles in *Common Ground*, although only the views of the authors, suggested indifferentism. Particular mention was made of an article by the historian Arnold Toynbee, which concluded with these words:

> In reality mankind has never been divided into an elect minority monopolising the light of God's countenance and a gentile majority sitting in outer darkness. There never has been any supernaturally privileged inner circle within the human family. The only treatment of history that is objective is one that treats all communities as equals; and this objective view of history is the only view that we can afford to present to our children in our now rapidly shrinking world.

Complaint was also made that a pamphlet, *Tolerance – Can it be Taught?*, had not been cleared by the Catholic authorities.[4] A subcommittee of CCJ, which examined these comments, reaffirmed that CCJ rejected indifferentism and felt that care had been taken to avoid this, but perhaps greater watchfulness was required.[5]

The Cardinal responded favourably to a personal initiative by Mr E. de Rothschild that some members of the Executive might meet with leading members of the Council to see if a way could be found to remove the Vatican's objections.

The press initially was slow to pick up the story. The first mention was in the *Universe* on 3 December 1954. Two weeks later, it was mentioned in the *Church of England Newspaper* and the *Jewish Chronicle*. After Christmas, the news was reported in the *Sunday Dispatch* and the *Sunday Express*, which, under the headline 'The Pope bans Queen's Council' was critical of Roman Catholic intolerance. Several dailies reported the news the next day. The most interesting article was in the *Tablet* on 1 January 1955. This accepted that some who had spoken under the Council's auspices might on occasion have elaborated views

> tending to indifferentism ... the general experience of Catholics taking part has been rather the opposite – that Catholics, Anglicans, Free Churchmen and Jews, finding themselves together as representative spokesmen for their beliefs, have earnestly sought, while being fully courteous, to be as truly representatives as they can of their own faiths.

Catholics had often been given the chance to explain about the persecution of Catholics in other parts of the world. It was pointed out that the ban did not apply to Catholics in other countries taking part in similar organisations. The *Tablet* then expressed the view that the 'public resignations could have been avoided' and further discussion should have been held. If then withdrawal really was necessary, the Vatican should have made its reasons clear. There was wide comment in the press on this article, which one paper said had 'caused a sensation in religious circles generally'.[6]

WHY?

Although the news came as a shock, it was not totally unexpected by those most intimately concerned with Council's affairs. It is hard now to recollect the mood before Vatican II and the famous decree *Nostra Aetate*, which Cardinal Hume has described as 'almost revolutionary'.[7] Archbishop Warlock, who had been on the staff of

Archbishop's House, Westminster at the time, said in 1981 that the Vatican instruction 'appears to have been based on false information', which he later said had been supplied by World Brotherhood.[8] World Brotherhood, a wider body for interfaith and international cooperation, was not by that date in existence. Dr Pierre Visseur, who was active in organising one of the earliest international conferences of Jews and Christians at Seelisberg in 1947, says that the opposition in Rome was headed by Cardinal Spellman, suspicious of American Jewish financial and political power.[9] As the Vatican records of that period are not yet available for historians, some uncertainty about what actually happened is bound to remain.

There had been earlier warnings of Rome's anxiety about CCJ. Even before the Seelisberg Conference, Simpson had been in touch with Professor Jacques Maritain, an outstanding Catholic thinker. Maritain had cautioned that the Catholic Church was suspicious of any kind of cooperation on a religious basis between Catholics, Protestants and Jews. The focus would need to be a common opposition to religious and racial persecution and that would have to include the sufferings of Catholics in Eastern Europe. Indeed in November 1947, the Cardinal nearly withdrew from CCJ on this matter. 'Why', Msgr Collingwood, the Cardinal's Private Secretary, asked of the Seelisberg Conference, 'should a conference be devoted entirely to Jewish affairs when a far more violent persecution of Christians is taking place in Eastern Europe?'[10] The Vatican, with a desire that the Holy Places in Jerusalem should be under international control, was also uneasy about developments in Israel/Palestine and did not (and still does not) recognise the State of Israel. Further, awareness of Christian complicity in antisemitism and therefore in Nazi horrors had hardly begun to dawn on Christians at the time.

In December 1950, two days before the Council's AGM, a message was received from Archbishop's House that the Cardinal would be unable to fulfil his promise to preside at the meeting. It was agreed to use the excuse of ill-health. In fact, a directive had been received from the Vatican instructing members of the hierarchy not to become associated with the International Council of Christians and Jews. It seems that this directive resulted from a report that the International Conference of Christians and Jews on Intergroup Education, held at Fribourg in August 1948, had shown tendencies to 'indifferentism' – the suggestion that one religion is as good as another.

In his reply, Simpson pointed out that attempts to form an International Council of Christians and Jews had come to nothing and that in any case great care had been taken with the abortive plans to ensure that neither the constitution nor the programme would imply 'indifferentism'. As no ICCJ was in existence, the directive could hardly have been taken to apply to CCJ, which had always repudiated indifferentism. Simpson's reply was sympathetically received and assurances were sent from Archbishop's House that efforts would be made to get clarification from the Vatican that the directive did not apply to CCJ.

Ironically, one reason why plans for ICCJ came to nothing was that despite his support at Fribourg, Everett Clinchy of the American National Conference of Christians and Jews, on his return to USA, advised NCCJ against supporting the embryonic body. Everett Clinchy subsequently put his energy into an organisation called World Brotherhood. This could have been regarded as 'indifferentist', which is not in everyone's vocabulary a pejorative term, but it is not clear that it ever came under the Vatican's ban.[11]

In the years after 1950, Simpson took great care to keep the Cardinal informed of CCJ's activities and also to distance CCJ from American and continental bodies which might arouse the Vatican's suspicions. It seems that when the directive to withdraw from CCJ was first received, the Cardinal called a meeting of Catholics who were deeply involved in CCJ's work. As a result a further letter was sent to the Vatican expressing dissent and asking for reconsideration. The subsequent reply merely confirmed the earlier instruction.

There is some suggestion that Cardinal Griffin himself was never particularly keen on the Council's work.[12] He would have liked it to give attention to wider problems of religious intolerance, for example to the persecution of Catholics in Northern Ireland or Eastern Europe. He was concerned that his withdrawal would not be misinterpreted by the Queen, who had become Patron of CCJ.

Despite official Roman Catholic withdrawal, CCJ continued to receive support from the *Tablet* and the sympathy of some Catholics. There are frequent references to the issue in correspondence throughout the 1950s. Simpson persisted in efforts to win back Catholic support. In 1956 he was in Rome and Norman St John-Stevas helped to get him an audience with Pope Pius XII.

Simpson made a little speech saying that he hoped the misunderstanding could be cleared up. The Pope, Simpson recalled, 'beamed on me with great warmth and pleasure and said, "This is a good work, I bless you in it" '.[13] With great delight, Simpson sent a message back to Edmund de Rothschild, then treasurer of CCJ. He was about to reply with a telegram of congratulations, when he discovered that there was indignation at Archbishop's House that Simpson should have gone over their heads and not applied for an audience through the proper channels.

In 1957, an enquirer asked the Catholic Information Centre about Catholic withdrawal from CCJ. The answer included the statement 'that it is not the custom of the Church to share a common platform in matters which may involve religious and ethical questions'.[14] The ban does not, however, seem to have been so rigorously applied in the USA.

ROMAN CATHOLICS REJOIN THE COUNCIL

By the early 1960s, with John XXIII as Pope, extensive changes were beginning to take place in the Roman Catholic Church, which came to their head at the Second Vatican Council. In a letter written in May 1961, Simpson mentions that the approaches initiated by Mr Edmund de Rothschild had reached the stage that the matter had been brought to the personal attention of the Pope, who had referred it to Cardinal Bea.[15] Later that year, in a television interview, Archbishop Heenan expressed regret about the decision to make Catholics withdraw from CCJ and said that many were working to get the decision, which he believed was founded on a mistake, reversed.[16] The following year the *Catholic Times* gave a favourable report of CCJ's AGM, mentioning that Archbishop Heenan had recently hinted that it was a field in which Catholics might soon cooperate again.[17] Shortly afterwards, approval was given for Catholic laymen, with the permission of their Bishop, to be associated with the Council and soon afterwards Mr L.F. Kelly once again took up his membership of the Council. In October, Lord Perth, whose father had been one of the original vice-presidents of CCJ, accepted an invitation to become a vice-president, and Lord Longford and Mr A.C.F. Beales became members of the Council.

In March 1964, Archbishop Heenan himself addressed the CCJ AGM and expressed his pleasure that Catholics were now again taking a full part in the life of the Council. He admitted that the withdrawal in 1954, on the orders of the Vatican, was partly because of a misunderstanding. Whilst still Archbishop of Liverpool, he had been to see Cardinal Ottaviani and asked him to remove this ukase. The Archbishop devoted the main part of his talk to discussions about the Jews then taking place at the Second Vatican Council.[18]

Archbishop Heenan implied that the Catholic return was because of his personal intervention with Cardinal Ottaviani. However, according to Archbishop Warlock, Cardinal Heenan wrote to the Vatican saying that if he did not hear from them by a certain date, he would assume his participation was all right. He never did hear.[19]

FURTHER DIFFICULTIES

Even now, it was not all calm sailing. Archbishop Roberts, who had been a bishop in India and whose disagreement with papal views about birth control had made him a controversial figure, was sympathetic to the Council. When he was in Rome, Archbishop Roberts tried, without success, to get at the roots of Vatican opposition. Consequently, when Catholics were again able to belong to the Council, Simpson invited him to join. Unfortunately, his affirmative reply was received on the very day that the *Evening Standard* published an article by Archbishop Roberts opposing the papal position on birth control. Cardinal Heenan, in a telephone call, threatened to resign if Roberts joined, but Roberts' membership escaped publicity and the matter dropped.

There were also some problems as to whether official Catholic approval had to be sought before a Catholic could be asked to speak at a CCJ meeting. In fact this issue was broadened when the question arose in 1966 about CCJ participation in or sponsorship of interfaith services. Simpson explained that the Council's policy had always been to avoid involvement in joint services, but, in the discussion, it became clear that there was resistance amongst some members to letting any outside body have a veto on the activities of CCJ. In 1967, the Catholic members of the Executive wrote to the chairman, Ven C. Witton-Davies, agreeing that it was sufficient for one of the Catholic members of the Executive to be consulted before a Catholic was invited to speak at a CCJ meeting. Local councils, which had considerable autonomy, were reminded of the need to ensure that any Catholics invited to speak were acceptable to the Catholic authorities, and encouraged to consult the Catholic members of the Executive, if necessary.[20]

Further difficulties, however, occurred when it was suggested that Dr Rijk, who was responsible at the Vatican for follow-up work in connection with the Declaration on the Church and the Jewish people, be invited to address the CCJ AGM in 1969. The idea was opposed at Archbishop's House. It seems that this was because Dr Rijk had disagreed with a statement made by Cardinal Heenan about the latter's ultimate interest in the conversion of Jews to Christianity.[21] It appears also that the Cardinal liked English Catholics to represent the Catholic Church at CCJ meetings and still saw the Council's primary work as opposing antisemitism. The issue also led to some tension between the office and officers. Unilateral action by certain of the honorary officers could put other officers and the staff in embarrassing positions. Eventually Dr Rijk had to be uninvited! In his place, Christopher Hollis, the chairman of the Cardinal's Commission on Relations with the Jews, was asked to speak at the AGM – some clear guidelines as to what he should say having been provided by Archbishop's House. In the course, however, of the correspondence between Archdeacon Witton-Davies and Msgr Norris, it was made clear that the Council could not accept a veto from an outside body.[22]

All this points to the somewhat ambiguous position of CCJ as an independent voluntary body, but with the co-sponsorship of the leaders of the Churches and of the Chief Rabbi, which gives the appearance to the public that the Council is an official organisation. I was particularly aware of this ambiguity when the Council wished to object to the visit of a Palestinian bishop to Lambeth Palace. The resistance to 'theological dialogue' by the Chief Rabbi and leaders of the Orthodox Jewish community raises similar questions.

A TRANSFORMATION

The difficulties between the Council and the Catholics for the first half of the Council's life have been quite transformed in recent years. As the Catholic Church has sought to implement *Nostra Aetate* and subsequent documents, Catholics have taken a very

4. Rev. W. W. Simpson with Teddy Kollek, Mayor of Jerusalem

5. Albert Polack (right) with Prime Minister Clement Attlee

6. Rev. Peter Jennings

active part in the work of CCJ. From 1969, Rev. Graham Jenkins, who is a Catholic deacon and who was then working at the bookshop at Westminster Cathedral, joined the Council and then the staff as organising secretary. His deep commitment to the cause for which the Council stands and his wide knowledge made him a very valuable member of staff and in all his work he was fully supported by his wife Phyl.

He was succeeded by Fr Roger Clarke, a Dominican priest, and then by Sister Margaret Shepherd, N.D.S., a Sister of Sion. Bishop Gerald Mahon, Bishop of West London, is now one of the vice-chairmen.

The warmth of relationships is emphasised by the fact that the Pope received a delegation from CCJ in both 1980 and 1990, and by the knighthood, as a member of the Equestrian Order of St Gregory, conferred on Sir Sigmund Sternberg, the joint honorary treasurer of CCJ and chairman of the International Council of Christians and Jews.

5

The Simpson Years

With the death of Henry Carter and Sir Robert Waley Cohen and the retirement of other founder members of CCJ, William Simpson's role became even more significant. Over the years his experience and his enormous number of contacts made the Council increasingly dependent on his knowledge and dedication. He remained general secretary from the Council's formation until 1974.

This is not, however, to underestimate the contribution that many others made to the life of the Council. Albert Polack made a distinguished contribution as education officer. He was succeeded in 1969 by C.D. Rappaport, who only stayed in this office until 1971. Both visited a great number of schools and colleges. Mr Wallace Bell, as organising secretary, sustained the administration and arranged many of the London area programmes. In 1962, he left to join the staff of Inter-Church Aid (better known as Christian Aid). He was followed by Rev. James Sexton, who stayed with the Council until 1970. For several years, Mr Sydney Nicklin was a conscientious finance officer.

In 1961, the staff was strengthened by the appointment of Mrs Joan Lawrence as assistant executive officer. She had previously worked in Cambridge as a psychiatric social worker. She soon assumed responsibility for CCJ's growing programme of publications. She brought a particular flair to the editorship of *Common Ground* and her literary ability was expressed through a variety of articles, short stories and a novel on the life of Moses, called *The Scapegoat*, which she wrote after her retirement. Joan, like Bill Simpson and Albert Polack, had a great gift for friendship, shown particularly in visits to local councils and at the annual summer conference. As Walter Bluhm put it in a tribute, Joan was 'not the power behind the throne, but the power next to it'.[1]

Although the office was always hard pressed because of the volume of work, the staff were well supported. Miss Walshaw, as secretary, devoted her life to the work of the Council. In addition, in 1957, for example, there were three other clerical staff and a telephonist.[2] The office was comfortably and conveniently situated at 41 Cadogan Gardens, in a house donated by a benefactor, Mr Reginald Graham.

The Council was well served by its honorary officers and Executive Committee members. After the death of Henry Carter, Charles Raven, who had just retired as Regius Professor of Divinity and Master of Christ's College at Cambridge, was invited to become chairman. Initially he refused because of his other commitments. Eventually the joint efforts of the Archbishop of Canterbury, of Cardinal Griffin and of the Chief Rabbi persuaded him to change his mind, although he was not free to take up his duties until he had completed his Gifford Lectures.

Although Canon Dillistone's biography of Charles Raven has only a passing mention of CCJ, the work was close to Raven's heart. It is true that he was neither a Hebraist nor an Old Testament scholar; however, a concern for reconciliation and unity was the passion of his life, shown for example in his commitment to the Fellowship of Reconciliation, his support for the World Congress of Faiths and his enthusiasm for Teilhard de Chardin, the French Catholic palaeontologist and priest, who wrote *Le Milieu Divin*. Raven's third wife was Hélène Jeanty, who because of her help to the Resistance had been taken prisoner by the Gestapo and held in a lunatic asylum in Germany. After the war, Hélène Jeanty devoted herself to helping refugees, especially those of an intellectual background.[3]

Charles Raven was a scholar of outstanding breadth and vision and often had new ideas about how the Council's work might develop. His Waley Cohen lecture on 'Tolerance and Religion' covers a wide canvas. Pointing out that the idea of tolerance is quite recent, he went beyond the need to remove prejudice, to suggest the positive enrichment that one could gain from learning about other traditions. 'If our co-existence is to become beneficial and creative, it must develop a sense of community, of positive partnership and mutual affection: and this involves a full degree of conscious cooperation not only in thought but in service'.[4] He gave, as an example, the contribution Jewish scholars were making to New

Testament studies. He also spoke of the coming together of the world religions and the challenge posed to all of them by scientific thought. Christians, he suggested, had to move away from old patterns of mission and replace them by dialogue. Together religions could contribute to the work of UNESCO, especially if they concentrated on social and ethical issues.

'If a Council like ours', he concluded,

> representing and uniting the two great religions of our Western world, could use its cooperative influence and personal friendships to explore and interpret the deeper and abiding elements of human community, the conditions of its attainment, and the character of its powers, we might make an essential contribution to the understanding and attainment not only of tolerance but of the family life of mankind which we both inherit and for which now at last the whole world is ready.[5]

He was succeeded by Carl Witton-Davies, Dean of St David's when he first joined the Council in 1953, although he had been a member of the Middle East Group since 1950. In 1957, now Archdeacon of Oxford, he was elected to the Executive, and elected chairman in 1958. This was a position that he retained until 1978. A Hebrew scholar and son of a professor of Hebrew, he had a deep love of the Holy Land and his enthusiasm for CCJ was boundless.

Other officers were active, especially Mr Edmund de Rothschild, the honorary treasurer. Mr Percy Bartlett was joint honorary secretary for 26 years, until he retired in 1968. Adolph Brotman, General Secretary of the Board of Deputies, who died in February 1970, was also a devoted joint honorary secretary in the early years.

The Council continued to receive strong backing from successive Archbishops of Canterbury and from the Chief Rabbis, Dr Brodie and then Dr Immanuel Jakobovits. The Moderators of the General Assembly of the Church of Scotland and of the Free Church Federal Council were also supportive. Their positions, however, were only held for a year, so it was hard for any of the Moderators to make the same impact on the Council as the Archbishop or Chief Rabbi.

At this period, of course, Roman Catholics had withdrawn their support. It is clear that this considerably weakened the Council and the issue absorbed a large amount of time. Even so, the work of the Council continued and in some measure grew.

COUNCIL EVENTS

A number of public events were arranged which conveyed the message of the Council or gave its work publicity. The Waley Cohen Lectures attracted distinguished speakers and large audiences. About 370 people attended the second lecture, held in 1955 at Middle Temple Hall, given by Professor Goodhart. Reports of the lecture appeared in *The Times*, the *Manchester Guardian* and the *Daily Telegraph*. The following year, the hall of the Inner Temple was crowded for Professor Herbert Butterfield's lecture on 'Toleration in British History'. The lecture in 1960 by the well-known psychiatrist Dr Stafford-Clark again attracted a very large audience of over 500 people. Some remarks he made expressing approval of inter-marriage brought criticism and the Council was quick to make clear that these were his personal views. Even more people came to the lecture in 1962 by Mr Abba Eban, who had represented Israel at the United Nations and was, for a time, its Foreign Secretary. His subject was 'The Final Solution – Reflections on the Jewish Tragedy', which was especially topical as the trial of Eichmann, who masterminded the Final Solution, was fresh in everyone's memory. Other distinguished lecturers attracted large audiences. In 1970, however, because of rising costs, which were defrayed by the generosity of the Waley Cohen family, the lecture became a biennial event.

To mark both the tenth and twentieth anniversaries of the Council, dinners were held at the Mansion House. On 8 October 1952, about 350 people attended the dinner. The speeches were given by Sir David Maxwell Fyfe, Archbishop Fisher, the Chief Rabbi, Mr Douglas Woodruff, Editor of the *Tablet*, and the Lord Mayor. Grace before dinner was said by Rev I. Levy, who was then Senior Jewish Chaplain to the Forces. The occasion was marked by a leader in *The Times*. It was at this time that the Queen kindly agreed to become patron of the Council.

A second dinner was held at the Mansion House on 12 October 1961. (There is always some debate about how to count anniversaries!). Two hundred and ninety guests attended. Speeches were made by Archbishop Michael Ramsey, Lord Radcliffe, the Chief Rabbi, Dr Israel Brodie, Dr Robert Birley, Headmaster of Eton, and the Lord Mayor. On both occasions, the dinners were followed by fund-raising efforts, which met with modest success.

In 1955, a luncheon was arranged at the House of Commons, at which the Archbishop of Canterbury presided. Because it was not possible to arrange a meal there that would fully meet the strict requirements of *kashrut*, the Chief Rabbi felt obliged to absent himself, although he expressed his good wishes for the success of the occasion. On a subsequent occasion in 1985, at a dinner at the Speaker's house, security precautions were lifted to allow a kosher meal to be brought into the Houses of Parliament. Another reception at the House of Commons, given by Sir Cyril and Lady Black, was held in 1962.

A particularly successful function was a Garden Party at Lambeth Palace held on 12 June 1956 to mark the 300th anniversary of the return of Jews to Great Britain. About one thousand guests attended who were 'representative of all sections of the national life'.[6] Local councils were well represented. The cost of catering was kept to 7/6d per head. The Salvation Army provided a band. A special brochure was produced. A small exhibition was arranged in the Lambeth Palace Library.

Another successful event, 'musically, socially and financially', was a concert to mark the 25th anniversary, held at the Royal Festival Hall in July 1967, in the presence of Her Majesty the Queen. The committee responsible for this had been ably headed by Lady Perth.[7] In the same year, at the Silver Jubilee annual meeting, the address was given by Dr Immanuel Jakobovits, newly installed as Chief Rabbi.

The Council's work was also made known through the press, through radio and through television. A special supplement to the *Jewish Chronicle* was produced in 1964. Simpson was invited from time to time to speak on 'Lift Up Your Hearts' and other radio programmes. In 1969, Simpson and Rev. Saul Amias took part in a television discussion, following a film of a Seder service held at Rosh Pinar Day School, Edgware. In June of the same year, Jewish and Christian choirs joined with an audience of members of the North West London Councils of Christians and Jews for a 'Songs of Praise'.

EDUCATIONAL WORK

Throughout this period the varied educational work of CCJ continued. An important project was a survey of history textbooks, with the aim of eliminating prejudicial remarks and attitudes. From time to time, in response to complaints, alleged prejudice was discussed with publishers. The quiet diplomatic approach of the Council usually gained a helpful response. For example, concern was voiced on more than one occasion about the 'Prioress' Tale' from Chaucer's *Canterbury Tales* being used as a set book.

There were the first signs of interest in teaching children about the great religions. With a few others, Bernard Cousins pioneered the way, with a memorandum in 1959, followed by his booklet *Introducing Children to World Religions*, in 1966. Professor Geoffrey Parrinder wrote some simple textbooks.

Conferences were arranged at various venues for teachers and some for schoolchildren. Mr Polack and other members of staff accepted a wide variety of speaking engagements. An exhibition was mounted at Westminster Abbey during its 'One People' Anniversary Year and, later, a travelling exhibition. The library was well used, although in the 1970s the sharp increase in postal charges hit all postal lending libraries. When the office moved to smaller accommodation, sadly, most of the library was disposed of.

A very useful part of the Council's educational programme has been an annual summer conference. The first was held in the early 1960s. These initially took place at a Cambridge college, but in recent years they have been held at Hengrave Hall, a beautiful Tudor mansion near Bury St Edmunds which is now a conference centre. These conferences have been especially appreciated by members who cannot easily take part in either London activities or in those of a local council. Many of the papers have been of a high standard and have been published in *Common Ground*.

RELIGIOUS FREEDOM

True to its remit to oppose all forms of discrimination, the Executive showed its concern about abuses of freedom in many parts of the world. The position of both Christian and Jewish believers in Eastern Europe was a constant worry. In 1953, for example, a protest was sent to the Czech Embassy about 'the extensive use of anti-Jewish and anti-Zionist arguments in the trial of fourteen former Communist leaders before a People's Court in Prague'.[8] In the same year, the Religious Liberty Group drew attention to the persecution of Protestants in Colombia, to the increase of anti-clericalism in Yugoslavia and the arrest of Cardinal Wyszynski in Poland, about whom an article appeared in *Common Ground*.[9]

The plight of Soviet Jews was a major concern. In April 1964, the Chief Rabbi voiced his worries at the annual meeting. Subsequently, the general secretary wrote to the Russian ambassador, mentioning especially the problems that Jews were having in obtaining unleavened bread. Simpson was also asked to broadcast on the subject on the BBC Third Programme. Four years later, the chairman wrote to the Foreign Office about the Council's concern. He was told, in reply, that the Prime Minister, during his recent visit to Moscow, had raised the matter, informally, with Mr Kosygin, but to little effect. In 1971, the Council shared in protests about the proceedings and sentences of the Leningrad Trial. The next year, whilst discussions of human rights were in progress, the Executive wrote to Sir Alec Douglas-Home about the bearing of the Universal Declaration of Human Rights on the position of Soviet Jews desiring to emigrate to Israel. In this, the Council worked closely with Keston College.[10]

The Executive felt that it was difficult for the Council to do much about the situation in South Africa, other than make clear, whenever possible, its opposition to the racism there. Ambrose Reeves, as Bishop of Stepney, served on the Executive before becoming Bishop of Johannesburg. In 1955, he was one of the speakers at the Annual Meeting. He explained his objections to the policy of compulsory segregation. The Very Rev. the Haham, a leader of the Sephardic community, also spoke at the meeting on 'Judaism and the Problems of Race Relations'. In 1971, the Council wrote to the South African ambassador protesting against the five-year sentence imposed on the Dean of Johannesburg, Very Rev. Gonville ffrench-Beytagh.[11]

The position of war orphans and especially the suggestion that some had been baptised by their foster-parents was taken up. Another matter was the possibility that Germany might default on payments of compensation to victims of Nazi oppression.

Another issue was the fate of Jews in Iraq. In January 1969, CCJ expressed its abhorrence of the hanging of Jews and others on alleged charges of spying. These protests were renewed after further hangings later that year and again in 1971.[12]

The Executive reacted strongly against the Commonwealth

Immigrants Bill of 1961. A statement was drafted which said that CCJ was

> deeply concerned with the moral and social issues raised by the bill and regretted that the Government felt it necessary to seek to control immigration of Commonwealth citizens. It believed that the problems addressed in the bill could have been tackled by long term measures to give greater economic assistance to Commonwealth territories and by vigorous action about social conditions, especially the lack of housing, in Britain.[13]

Not all members were happy about CCJ taking such a political stand. In the end no public statement was made, although the Council recorded its deep concern about the underlying racial tension, which had provoked the bill, and about the bill's implications. The Executive reaffirmed 'the Council's belief that any form of discrimination on grounds of race or colour is contrary to the fundamental principles of Judaism and Christianity alike and as such a danger to the best interests of any human society'.[14] The joint presidents welcomed the action of the Executive and the Moderator of the Church of Scotland said he was glad no public statement had been made, 'as to have done so would have committed, at least by implication, the Presidents of the Council on a matter involving party politics'.[15] Once again, it was clear how thin a tightrope the Council has to tread.

In 1971 a new Immigration Bill came before Parliament and, at the request of local councils, the Executive again discussed the matter. It was suggested that a letter might be written to the Home Secretary, particularly stressing the need for long-term educational work in community relations if the problems of a pluralistic society were to be satisfactorily overcome. There was again concern lest the Council became too political.[16] Yet, by avoiding anything that could appear political, the Council could be rendered impotent, only able to mouth acceptable platitudes and generalities.

It is impossible to estimate the effect of protest and statements. Few governments acknowledge the pressures upon them – least of all totalitarian regimes. Yet, it is always important that violations of human rights are denounced. This witnesses that there is a moral conscience in the world, of which religious communities are rightly the guardians. Comment too can help to inform public opinion.

ANTISEMITISM

The Notting Hill riots in 1958 came as a shock to the nation. At an early stage in the troubles, the warden of the North Kensington Community Association invited Simpson to a private meeting. Prior to this meeting, Mr Wallace Bell drew up a memorandum on some of the causes of the riots and possible approaches to a solution. Subsequently a copy of the memorandum was sent to the mayors of neighbouring boroughs. When the Mayor of Kensington set up a working party, CCJ was represented on it. Indeed, CCJ was the only national body to be part of this group, and probably at the time few organisations had as much experience as the Council in trying to reduce prejudice and racial hatred.[17]

The Executive was quick to react to any sign of antisemitism. In 1958, a Fascist meeting was planned to be held in the Guildhall at Northampton. The local British Legion, local clergy and CCJ nationally were amongst those who protested and the authorities in Northampton subsequently cancelled the booking.[18]

In 1962, the National Socialist Movement announced a public rally in Trafalgar Square to 'Free Britain from Jewish control'. It was agreed that Archdeacon Witton–Davies, Chairman of CCJ, should write to the Lord Chancellor. The Minister of Works in reply said that no political censorship was exercised over those arranging a public meeting. In the event the gathering was held on 1 July, but was stopped early by the police because of the disorder that had broken out.[19]

This event led to some discussion on the Executive and with the Chief Rabbi and the Archbishop about the possible need for legislation on the subject of discrimination and incitement against groups. A letter was sent to the Home Secretary calling for vigilance and consideration of ways of preventing similar demonstrations. In his reply, the Home Secretary, the Rt Hon. Henry Brooke, said he would consider the possibility of amending the Public Order Act. In due course, legislation has been introduced to curb incitement to racial hatred, but not to religious hatred, although the Salman Rushdie affair has brought the latter to public notice. It is interesting to note that in 1968 the Hampstead CCJ sent a letter to their Member of Parliament, Mr Ben Whitaker, suggesting that the Race Relations Bill, then before Parliament, should be extended to prohibit discrimination on the grounds of religion. At the Executive discussion, Sir Barnett Janner supported this view.[20] The proper concern to preserve personal freedom has made British society slow to curb the abuse of that freedom. Jewish authorities too have often found government officials slow to take action against prejudicial literature.

The 1962 discussions again raised the question of the appropriate response for CCJ to make to such events. The Executive decided against making a public statement, although the newly formed North London council had asked it to do so. The editorial of *Common Ground* was devoted to the subject, but some members of CCJ and indeed some members of the Executive clearly thought CCJ should have been more forthright. The need to keep together a wide coalition could lead to caution, lest someone were to be offended.[21]

A recurring issue was *shechita*. The Royal Society for the Prevention of Cruelty to Animals raised objections from time to time and there were also some moves to introduce legislation in Parliament. The Council consistently maintained that it was as humane a method of slaughter as other methods allowed by law and produced some pamphlets explaining *shechita*.[22]

Thanks to the efforts of CCJ, dictionaries gradually revised their definition of 'Jew', removing the more opprobrious meanings.[23] Again, because of CCJ's intervention in 1968, the York *Official Guide* revised a paragraph about Clifford's Tower which was ambiguous and open to misinterpretation.[24] The Radio and TV Group was always alert to challenge prejudicial comments, whilst the Religious Press Club helped to build up positive images.

Some discrimination is more subtle. Certain golf clubs used to have restrictive admission policies. In 1952, in response to complaints, the Secretary of the English Golf Union wrote:

> The game of golf in many cases is merely incidental to the Club life, and it is true that in some cases clubs prefer to exclude Jewish members, while in other clubs where Jewish members predominate they too prefer to have membership restricted to persons of their own religion. The Union is in no position to take official cognisance of these matters which in the view of my Committee do not necessarily involve racial or religious discrimination that is inconsistent with the best interests of British sportsmanship.

Some members of the Executive took exception to the reference to clubs where Jewish members predominate.[25] Subsequent minutes show that in several clubs admission was by open vote. Note was taken of the decision of one town council to terminate the licence of a club because of alleged incidents of antisemitism.

Restrictive admission policies to some boys' and girls' independent public and preparatory schools was another concern and was the subject of an article in the *Evening Standard*. The 1954 autumn issue of *Common Ground* contained an article on the subject. Copies, with a covering letter, were sent to the heads of many independent schools.[26] It seems that this helped to change attitudes at several schools. The Council also pressed for the admission of Carmel College, a school for Jewish boys, to the Headmasters' Conference.[27]

ANTI-JUDAISM

It is at first glance surprising how little evidence of concern for anti-Judaism appears in the Executive records in the 1950s and early sixties. There is objection to obviously prejudicial attitudes. A complaint was made, for example, about the broadcast of R.F. Delderfield's 'Spark in Judaea', which showed Pontius Pilate in a flattering light. There was another complaint from a Jewish family about a New Testament story by a popular author which they had found in their local library. In response to CCJ's complaint, the author wrote to the family and the library withdrew the book.[28]

There was little mention of the Holocaust. The shock was still too recent and too great. There was therefore small recognition at that time of the Christian share of responsibility for Jewish suffering. It was not until 1961 that the World Council of Churches repudiated accusations of deicide and the Vatican Council's *Nostra Aetate* only dates from 1965.

In 1961, a concentration camp exhibition was staged in Coventry and subsequently in some other cities and in London. One might have expected the Council to support this, but Simpson told the organisers that CCJ could not officially be associated with the exhibition. Simpson, however, did correspond with the Provost of Coventry, who felt the exhibition was likely to perpetuate hatred and bitterness. When the exhibition was staged at Manchester, Manchester CCJ decided against giving any support to the project.[29]

It is interesting also that the suggestion that the Ten Points of Seelisberg be reprinted, with a brief commentary, was turned down. It was felt 'inappropriate for the Council to publish a pamphlet on this difficult subject in this form at the present time ... The subject needed such expert treatment as might be given by members of the Divinity Faculty of a University'. It was considered sufficient, if there were enquiries, to refer people to an earlier copy of *Common Ground*, where the Ten Points had been printed, without commentary.[30]

A hint of the changes ahead was the agreement to Dr Parkes' request to help finance the publication of his translation of Professor Jules Isaac's essay on 'Antisemitism: Has it Christian Roots?' which, with Parkes' own work, was a pioneering effort in this field.[31] Another hint was the publication in 1961 of Paul Winter's *The Trial of Jesus*. Professor Trevor-Roper's review in the *Sunday Times* led to quite a lot of correspondence.[32] In *Common Ground*, where the articles were by individual contributors, there was rather more discussion of the theological issues.

Another sign of a growing awareness of the theological issues was an initiative of the London Council for Christian–Jewish Understanding. Inspired by George Appleton, then Vicar of St Botolph's, who was on the Executive of CCJ and who was later to become Anglican Archbishop in Jerusalem, the Council asked the Archbishop of Canterbury for a pre-Easter statement. In this Dr Ramsey said:

> it is always wrong when people try to lay the blame upon the Jews for the crucifixion of Jesus Christ. In the event the Roman Governor was no less responsible for what happened. The important fact, however, is that the crucifixion was the clash between the Love of God and the sinfulness and selfishness of the whole human race. Those who crucified Christ are in the true mind of the Christian Church representatives of the whole human race, and it is for no one to point a finger of resentment at those who brought Jesus to his death, but rather to see the crucifixion as the divine judgment upon all humanity for choosing the ways of sin rather than the Love of God. We must all see ourselves judged by the crucifixion of Christ.[33]

For many years, each Holy Week, the London Council reminded Christians through the church press of this teaching, whilst in

1971 CCJ issued a background paper on problems associated with traditional presentations of the Passion story.[34] George Appleton also persuaded the London Council to start an annual St Paul's lecture on a topic of interest to Jews and Christians.[35]

By 1969, the Council was ready to publish a leaflet on *Christian teaching and Antisemitism*, which was widely distributed. A request was also received from the United Evangelical and Lutheran Churches in Germany for permission to translate it. Later that year the important booklet *Facing Realities*, which Rabbi Raymond Apple, who is now in Sydney, helped to prepare, was published by CCJ. This included summaries of the new approaches of both the Catholic Church and of the World Council of Churches. It also reprinted the Ten Points of Seelisberg.[36]

The changing mood is shown by comparing the muted reaction in 1960 to the Oberammergau Passion play with the considerable controversy that preceded the 1970 production. Archdeacon Witton-Davies went to the play in 1960 and said that 'he had been very impressed with the performance and did not feel that there was any serious ground for complaint in what was after all an attempt to represent the story as recorded in the Gospels'. This view was also supported by Mr Wallace Bell, the organising secretary.[37]

Ten years later feelings towards the play were more critical. It was discussed by the Standing Committee of European Rabbis and at the CCJ Executive. As the Oberammergau community rejected suggestions of revising the text, a number of people boycotted the play. Inter-Church Travel, however, drew people's attention to a statement by Cardinal Suenens' Ecumenical Officer, which is very remarkable for so quickly going further than *Nostra Aetate*. The statement made clear that the play belonged to the tradition of antagonism, which had been shamelessly used to justify massive manslaughter.

> All who attend it should bear in mind that while the origin of the Play at Oberammergau lies in a popular sentiment, the actual understanding and interpretation of it needs to be corrected towards justice and truth in the light of biblical, theological and sociological knowledge. No Jews in our days are responsible for the death of our Saviour, nor were all Jews of his time. In all countries there are, and have been people able and willing to perpetrate the worst crimes. The Jews who

shouted, 'His blood be upon us ...' are representatives of the evil persons everywhere, always, for whom our crucified Lord prayed, 'Father, forgive them, for they know not what they are doing.' Of course, the great majority of the Jewish people had no part in the events of the Passion and a number of them were already followers of Christ or ready to become members of a flock which can be called the Church of the Day of Pentecost.[38]

ISRAEL

There was also limited discussion of Israel at Executive meetings. The Middle East Group, however, did meet regularly and undertook detailed studies of the question of Jerusalem and the Holy Places, of Arab refugees and of German reparations. There was a feeling that Israel was sometimes unfairly blamed for the plight of the Arab refugees. It was noted that it was Israel's Arab neighbours who refused to make peace.[39]

Considerable shock was caused in 1953 when a group of Israelis attacked the village of Quibya, close to the Jordan border, and killed 53 inhabitants. It was at once recognised that this was a political matter and outside the Council's competence. There was, however, concern about the effect of the news on Christian–Jewish relations in Britain. A call for constructive peace efforts was, therefore, made at the next AGM.[40]

The Suez crisis in 1956 occasioned deep anxiety and an emergency meeting of the Executive was called. Again, the Council's primary concern was the effect upon relations between Christians and Jews in Britain. It was felt that generous treatment of Arab refugees by the Israelis would be a healing factor.[41]

Great excitement was caused by an invitation to CCJ, made in 1958, by the External Relations Department of the Jewish agency and of the Ministry of Religious Affairs in Israel, to send a delegation of Christian leaders to the country. Discussions and plans took up a large part of subsequent meetings – we today so easily take international travel for granted. The delegation eventually set out on 23 September 1958. After a few days in Lebanon and Jordan, the group entered Israel on 30 September. At a special meeting on 2 December, the group reported on their visit. In Lebanon and Jordan, where they met mostly Christian leaders, they found that the problem of Arab refugees dominated everything else. Privately some locals were prepared to admit that Israel was a permanent reality. In general, the group found that 'there was complete lack of understanding on the Arab side of how Jews think and feel about the establishment of a Jewish State in the land of Zion'. The group wondered whether the Churches had any role to play in interpreting each side to the other. In Israel, the party was impressed by the realistic way in which immigrants were being assimilated. They noted that there was complete religious liberty for all recognised communities.[42]

Almost immediately afterwards, the Council heard of the formation of a Committee for Inter-Faith Understanding in Israel, headed by Dr Benjamin Mazar, the President of the Hebrew University. Good wishes were sent to the new committee, and CCJ has over the years kept in close touch with interfaith developments in Israel.[43]

The Six Days War in 1967 at once demanded the attention of the Executive. Again, it was careful to avoid political comment. It is interesting to see how soon it was felt that public sympathy had moved away from Israel, which had captured Jerusalem and had occupied the West Bank. A pamphlet, *Arabs and Jews in the Middle East; A Tragedy of Errors* was quickly prepared by James Parkes. Some of his views, in later years, on the situation in Israel caused offence in some Jewish circles. 'He nevertheless conceived it his duty to propagate his ideas, however unpopular, fortified in the knowledge that, as an esteemed "honorary Jew", his friends would appreciate a candid assessment of the situation as he saw it'.[44]

By early the following year, the Executive was criticising a British Council of Churches' report on 'The Agony of Jerusalem'. Whilst the article rightly tried to gain sympathy for the Arab refugees, it was thought quite unfair to the attitudes and actions of the Israeli authorities. Sadly such disagreements about the Middle East between Christians in Britain have recurred, perhaps inevitably, since those working with refugees are likely to identify with their view of their plight, whereas those closely in touch with the Jewish community will be more aware of Israeli insecurity and the country's problems and divisions.[45]

Over the years there was talk about a CCJ joint Christian and Jewish tour to Israel. This encountered many difficulties. Prior to 1967, Jordan was not prepared to admit the group. Eventually this took place in October 1969. Twenty-four people took part. One week was spent in Jerusalem and the second week in Galilee, where the group stayed at both an Orthodox and a secular kibbutz.

An issue that caused some difficulties was missionary activity in Israel. There were reports, which distressed some Christians, of curbs being placed on Christian missionaries by Israeli authorities. CCJ's enquiries showed that the reports in general were not true, as the Israeli government respected religious freedom, but there was some attempt to protect children from unwanted proselytism. There was also quite a lot of public resentment in Israel against missionaries. CCJ itself was not particularly sympathetic to missionary activity, but was concerned for religious freedom.[46]

SHARED MORAL INSIGHTS

From the beginning, one hope had been that the Council might witness to the shared moral insights of Judaism and Christianity. A repeated theme was Toleration and several of the Waley Cohen lectures were on the subject.

There was some discussion of the morality of nuclear weapons at one of the sub-committees.[47] The 1971 Conference was about the environment, which is not an invention of the late eighties!

In 1963, after considerable preparation and discussion, Manchester CCJ caused a stir by suggesting that a world conference of Christian and Jewish leaders should be convened and also a world conference of Christian and Muslim leaders. Nothing came of this.[48]

TOO MANY DEMANDS

The persistent problem which has faced the Council appeared quite early in its life. With such a vast remit and with a very small staff and resources, how was the Council to be most effective? Longer-term educational work requires considerable planning and often its fruits are not seen for several years. As a result it may not appear attractive to potential donors who look for quick results. Equally it may be eclipsed and interrupted by some sudden crisis in Christian Jewish relations. Very easily the immediate diverts attention from longer-term work. Equally, energies can be too diversified and what seems a good idea at a committee meeting is not adequately costed in terms of time and money before a decision is made whether or not to implement it.

In a review in 1956, partly brought on by financial problems, it was recognised that the development and strengthening of local councils and an increase in publications should be priorities. As so often these developments, which it was thought would strengthen the Council and therefore attract additional funds, needed funds to be initiated. The 1956 programme required an additional £10,000. It was noted that unlike most charities the Council had no one employed with primary responsibility for fund-raising. It appears that not much was done about the recommendations.[49]

A report dated March 1957 gives an interesting picture of the job responsibilities of members of staff. It recognised that there was no rigid separation of duties, but gave these job descriptions.

> The General Secretary: Ultimate responsibility to the Executive Committee for the Council's work: relations with other organisations: development of work with clergy and ministers, and theological colleges; contact with local councils.
>
> Organising Secretary: Arrangement of speakers, etc, for meetings in London and the Home Counties area; press and publications; finance and membership; general administration of office.
>
> Education Officer: Work in schools, teachers' training colleges and universities.[50]

Then, as throughout its history, it has been amazing how much such a small staff achieved.

There was another review in 1969, largely because of a deteriorating financial position. Rapid inflation was making it hard to attract adequate funds – most of which still came from individual Jewish donors. The report's suggestion was to cut back the work by stopping the publication of *Common Ground* and also by reducing the number of staff. It was recommended that either the Publications Officer or the Education Officer and their respective part-time assistant should be made redundant.

These recommendations were resisted by Simpson. He pointed out that to lose either officer was bound to weaken the educational work of the Council, which was its very *raison d'être*. The overheads of maintaining the organisation would be much the same, but its work and effectiveness reduced. He argued that the Council should think in terms of increasing its income to do its necessary work. He pointed out that two plans for fund-raising had been 'quietly pigeon-holed without any action being taken' . He spoke also of the staff's 'constant sense of frustration, not least because we have been expected to operate a programme which could do little to impress potential supporters with any sense of the relevance of the Council's work to some of the major issues confronting the community at the present time'. Simpson, who could see the possibilities of the Council, obviously felt hampered by the many hesitations, whether the fear of being political or of upsetting the Roman Catholics or some other religious group, and by the lack of finance for any new initiative. Indeed, some of the officers seemed mainly con-cerned to cut back activities and to use the Council as a means to secure influential contacts.[51]

The following years saw heated discussion about the way forward and how to finance it. Economies were made to *Common Ground*, but the journal survived. When Charles Rappaport resigned as Education Officer, he was not replaced for some time. The years immediately prior to Simpson's and Joan Lawrence's retirements, in 1974, were sadly ones of cutback. Simpson too had personal problems to worry him.

When he did resign, however, proper acknowledgment of his immense services to CCJ were made. He was given the title of General Secretary Emeritus and continued to make his unique contribution to Christian Jewish relations in Britain. He was also free to devote his energies to building up the infant International Council of Christians and Jews, in which work he was ably assisted by Ruth Weyl. He became ICCJ's honorary chairman and, from 1981, he became an honorary life vice-president.

W. W. SIMPSON

On William Wynn Simpson's retirement, many tributes were paid to him. The farewell occasion was planned for the Jerusalem Chamber at Westminster Abbey, but so many people wanted to come that it was moved to the old Foundling Hospital. After he had lit the Hanukkah candle, the Chief Rabbi described W.W.S. as the 'shamos', who had given light and fire to the five joint Presidents. An antique brooch was presented to Mrs Winifred Simpson.[52]

James Parkes paid him a fulsome tribute in *Common Ground* – although admittedly Parkes said more about himself than about Bill! He mentions Simpson's exposed position. 'W.W. was obliged to accept the slings and arrows of outrageous ecclesiastical bureaucracy – I am not suggesting that all his ecclesiastical contacts deserved such condemnation – and endeavour with saintly patience to guide them into better ways.'[53] Parkes, besides mentioning the well-deserved OBE, pointed particularly to Bill's broadcasting technique and popular style of writing. He also mentioned his unfailing concern to foster international work. Besides playing an active part in the committee of the European Councils of Christians and Jews and participating in various meetings of the World Council of Churches, he was active in the Christian Peace Conference and attended its meetings in Moscow and Prague. Simpson was also a member of a wide range of other charitable and peace-loving bodies, including the World Congress of Faiths, the Pestalozzi Children's Village, the Greater London Association for the Disabled of which he was a vice-president, and the National Council of Social Service, of which for some time he was the advisory secretary to the Central Churches Group. Besides the inherent value of the work of these organisations in which Simpson was involved, through them he made a wide range of contacts for CCJ, thereby helping to extend its influence.

Simpson's interest in the work continued until the end of his life, with the enthusiastic support of his companion Ruth Weyl. In July 1987 he attended the ICCJ Colloquium, which was held in Switzerland and which commemorated the fortieth anniversary of the Seelisberg Conference. A fortnight before his death, which occurred on 29 August 1987, a letter of his appeared in the *Jewish Chronicle*, in reply to a complaint that there had been little change in Christian attitudes towards Jews. 'Remembering how long it has taken us to get into the tangle of relationships in which we find ourselves today, the miracle is that so much progress has been made towards their disentanglement in so relatively short a time.'[54] Just after I heard of his death, I opened the new issue of *Theology*, to find there another letter from Simpson. It ended with the words, 'We journey through the Egyptian-black night, but into day.'[55] Simpson, in a remarkable way, helped to lead the Churches and the Jewish community from the black night of Nazism into the new day of Christian dialogue and understanding.

Members of every section of the Jewish and Christian communities paid tribute to his memory at a moving memorial gathering held in the Great Hall of King's College, London. Perhaps, however, the most fitting tribute was paid, on his retirement, by Walter Bluhm, in a poem called 'A Mensch', from which I quote the final verse:

It is the little something
which builds bridges
from alpha unto omega
that little extra
the God-inspired gift
which unites mankind
the bonus of God's grace
which makes the common man
into a Mensch
the Mensch you've always been
the Mensch you are.

6

The Struggle to Survive

It is almost part of the ritual of the annual meetings of voluntary organisations for the treasurer to speak of the urgent need for more money and for someone else to deplore the lack of young people. Worries about money throughout the 1970s were, sadly, no meaningless ritual but a dire necessity. At a time of rapid inflation, CCJ, along with other voluntary bodies, faced serious problems.

The annual reports and *Common Ground* are full of this concern. The cover of the summer issue for 1976 is headed 'Help'. It explains the need to increase subscriptions and appeals for donations. Inside on the first page, there is a notice headed 'Finis?' This warned that unless new money was found, this would be the last issue of *Common Ground* in its present form. This warning led to some generous donations, so that an autumn issue of *Common Ground* was published. Sadly, sufficient money was not available for any issues to be published in 1977, but *Common Ground* reappeared in 1978. Another indication of the seriousness of the situation was the fact that at one time there was no money to pay staff salaries, until the situation was remedied, at least temporarily, by one individual's generosity.[1] Indeed the annual report of 1975–6 spoke of it as a year 'which saw the Council in its most precarious situation since its inception'.[2]

Thanks to the determination and courage of the staff and of the Executive, who 'were convinced that the work of the Council is on-going',[3] plans were soon being made for a major appeal. The figure was originally set at £250,000, although quickly increased to £295,000. Sir Sigmund Sternberg, who has played such an energetic role in the life of the Council, became Appeal Chairman and then joint honorary treasurer. He was soon able to announce that promises of about £100,000 had been made. Dr Donald Coggan, then Archbishop of Canterbury and a joint president, welcomed this news at the 1977 annual meeting. It was a 'fine start', which he hoped would lead to a 'flying finish'.[4]

A number of special events were arranged. Perhaps the most splendid was the Royal Silver Jubilee Concert at Westminster Abbey on 1 December 1977. This was held in the presence of H. M. Queen Elizabeth, the Queen Mother. Yehudi Menuhin and his school orchestra gave their services. A noteworthy aspect of the concert was the sponsorship of seats for some blind and some disabled people. Special transport to and from the Abbey was arranged for them and they were provided with meal boxes at the end of the concert. The successful organisation was headed by Mr Edmund de Rothschild, who, as honorary treasurer, had done so much for the Council over the years. His daughter, Miss Charlotte de Rothschild, presented a bouquet to the Queen Mother. The concert raised over £10,000.

Luncheons, hosted respectively by one of the joint presidents, also attracted new interest in the Council and were useful in their contributions to the fund-raising.

STAFF

The financial difficulties were also met by severe cutbacks. During 1975, both W. W. Simpson and Joan Lawrence left the staff. The new general secretary was Rev. Peter Jennings.

Peter Jennings was born in Manchester on 9 October 1937 and was educated at Manchester Grammar School. At Oxford, he read classics and theology and then studied for the Methodist ministry at Hartly Victoria Methodist College, Manchester. It was during his training at Manchester that his great interest in the Hebrew Bible was kindled. During his time there, he took an M.A. in Semitic Studies. He also heard a lecture from Bill Simpson about CCJ. His probationer post was in Swansea, where he became a member of the executive of Swansea CCJ. It was there also that he got to know Len Goss (see below). After being ordained in 1965, he moved to London in 1967 to become Tutor Warden of the Social Studies Centre of the London Circuit (East) of the Methodist Conference and was deeply involved with youth work in a very ethnically mixed community. His interest in CCJ continued to grow and he became a member of the executive of North London CCJ. Peter was to continue as general secretary until the end of 1981. He then became director of the Whitechapel Mission. His interest in the work of CCJ has continued, especially through his leadership of the North London CCJ and as a chairman of the Standing Conference of Local Councils. He also heads the British Friends of Nes Ammim, a pioneering Christian community in Israel.

In 1975, Peter Jennings was joined at CCJ headquarters by Leonard Goss. Len was born in London in 1925. As a boy he joined the Scouts and continued to be active in this movement throughout his life. He was the secretary of the first Youth Synagogue to be formed in Britain, which was sponsored by the Jewish Memorial Council in London's East End. He was a devout Orthodox Jew. When he moved to Swansea, he soon became honorary secretary of the Swansea Hebrew Congregation, where he sometimes conducted the children's services. For 15 years he was the prime mover in the Swansea Jewish Junior Club. He also became a leading member of the Swansea branch of the International Friendship League and this lead to widespread travel. Len was a member of a large range of voluntary and communal activities – very often as an officer or committee member. A vivacious person, he had an enormous number of acquaintances. He began his working life as a journalist and became news editor of the *South Wales Evening Post*. In 1970, he took an administrative job at the University College of Swansea.

When he joined the staff of CCJ in 1975, he had already been a member for 25 years. He had also been an office-holder from the formation of Swansea CCJ. He was appointed as organising secretary, but was soon also involved in education, publications, supporting local councils, as well as in fund raising. After a time, he became joint chief executive officer with Peter Jennings. In 1978, Len married Miss Mildred Gershon, who later was to become office secretary. When Peter Jennings left CCJ, Len Goss became general secretary, with Rev. Deacon Graham Jenkins as organising secretary. Early in the 1980s, with the hope of expanding the activities of the Council, partly as a result of a generous grant from the Group Relations Educational Trust, it was decided to appoint an Executive Director. Len graciously accepted this development, himself becoming Administrative Director.

Initially it was hoped that Rev. Eric Allen, a minister of the United Reformed Church, who was deeply involved in Jewish Christian dialogue, would accept the post of Executive Director. In the end this did not prove possible for him, although later he took on his present position as joint honorary secretary of the Council. When I took up the position of Executive Director in July 1984, Len Goss had been leading CCJ for three and a half years. All too soon, he was taken ill at the 1984 annual meeting and died at the end of the year. His widow, Mildred, who had come to share his experience and wide knowledge of the work, has continued as secretary at CCJ and is known to many members.

During much of their time at CCJ, Peter Jennings and Len Goss bravely maintained the work of the Council, which in earlier years had been done by a staff of at least double the size. With the uncertainties about funding, together with a period in which, whilst moving between offices, they had to operate from their homes, their courage and dedication deserves to be recognised. They kept alive the work of the Council during a difficult period.

In 1978, they were joined by Anne Cecilia Baring as part-time education officer. A devout Roman Catholic, she has a deep love of Judaism and a profound knowledge of Israel, which she has visited on many occasions. For ten years, she was headmistress of a girls' school. She has also an active interest in the Girl Guides and the Brownies. As education officer, she travelled very widely, speaking at a great number of schools and colleges, sharing with them her unrivalled collection of visual aids. She stayed with the Council until the autumn of 1983, although she has continued her wide ranging educational work on a free-lance basis. Mr Lionel Slavid, who had had wide experience at the Inner London Education Authority (ILEA), had by then become, on a voluntary basis, joint education officer and has continued his concern for CCJ's educational work.

Rev. Graham Jenkins, a Roman Catholic deacon, became organising secretary in 1981 and continued this work until 1987. He had previously been manager of the bookshop at Westminster Cathedral and had an unrivalled knowledge of the literature on Christian–Jewish issues. He had been on CCJ's executive since 1969. For some time, Graham Jenkins was honorary secretary of the Catholic Commission on Christian–Jewish Relations. He has also been an active member of the Rainbow Group. With his wife

Phyl, who is equally enthusiastic about the work, he has led many parties to Israel. Through his writing and his talks to a wide variety of audiences, Graham Jenkins has made an invaluable contribution to improving Christian–Jewish relations, a task which he has seen as his vocation.

In 1976, Sydney Nicklin, who had been finance officer from 1963 to 1975, died. He had given himself with great devotion to the work of CCJ. Others who helped with the necessary financial work were Mrs Joan Durney and Mrs Hilda Wells. In 1978, Mr Ian Scott was appointed finance officer, joining CCJ from another charity. In 1983, he was succeeded by David Loftus, who had served in the army and who eventually took up work with the Children's Society. In 1978, there were two office secretaries, Miss Robyn Sheer and Mrs Kay Miles and for a time, to help out, Mrs Queenie Weber, an active member of Finchley CCJ, did part-time work in the office. The activities of the office staff may be less 'newsworthy', but their work is indispensable and CCJ, like many other charities, can be grateful to those who gave of themselves to the cause far 'above the call of duty'.

OFFICERS

In 1978 Carl Witton-Davies retired as chairman of the Executive, a position that he had held with distinction for 20 years. Thanking him for his service, Archbishop Coggan said, 'I have a strong suspicion that the work and witness of this Council probably takes precedence over all his many interests.'[5] Carl himself said that

> in many years within the Church of England – and I cannot resist adding the Church in Wales – as well as in the broader field of inter-religious dialogue opened to me through my work in the Holy Land and then in CCJ, I cannot claim to have found any organisation more worthy of support, bringing as it does, the best of Christianity and Judaism to bear on the problems of the day, whether they be racial, religious or moral.[6]

In recognition of his services, Witton-Davies was presented, in 1979, with the first Sir Sigmund Sternberg Award for a distinguished contribution to Christian–Jewish relations. These awards, which were to become an annual event, helped to give a higher profile to the Council's work, as well as being an acknowledgment of remarkable service.

His successor was Canon Douglas Webster, who for some years was on the staff of the London College of Divinity and then became Education Secretary of the Church Missionary Society. From 1966 to 1969 he was Professor of Mission at the Selly Oak Colleges, Birmingham. In his Canterbury Cathedral lecture, he welcomed the approach of dialogue. Christians, he said, 'must scrupulously lay aside every hint of superiority and arrogance ... We must have a willingness to learn from each other and to embrace new truths, from whatever quarter they come.'[7] Canon Webster was the author of several books and was a fluent communicator as well as world traveller. In 1969 he became a Residentiary Canon of St Paul's Cathedral, London. In the early 1960s, the World Council of Churches asked him to do a survey throughout the Middle East. He visited Israel then as he had done before and was to do again.

Canon Douglas Webster stressed the value of CCJ in enabling members of the two religions to oppose prejudice. In an article which he wrote for *Common Ground*, he said that he longed for Christianity and Judaism,

> which have a common heritage and a common goal, to work together with mutual respect and trust, in fighting some of the evils around us, especially intolerance and prejudice, whether racist or religious. So much of this is fostered by lies and results in senseless cruelty ... The great prophets ... campaigned against lies and did their utmost to expose them. We need to do this still, today more than ever, for neither the Nazis in the '30s nor the National Front in the '70s could survive even for a few weeks except on a diet of lies. And lies always breed hatred and cruelty. I want to stretch out hands of fellowship to all who will fight cruelty in whatever form we find it – cruelty to the old, cruelty to children, cruelty to blacks, cruelty to minorities, cruelty to the mentally handicapped, cruelty to the poor and hungry, cruelty to prisoners, especially prisoners of conscience.[8]

Sadly, especially towards the end of his time in office, Canon Webster suffered from serious illness. When he moved away from London to Gloucestershire, he retired from the chairmanship. His position was taken in 1983 by the Right Rev. Lord Coggan, who in 1980 had retired from being Archbishop of Canterbury.[9]

In 1978, the same year that Archdeacon Witton-Davies retired, so also did Martin Savitt who had been an active joint honorary secretary for several years. He was succeeded by Rev. Dr Isaac Levy, generally known as 'Harry', who had been Senior Chaplain to the Forces and who was rabbi of the Hampstead Synagogue. He had already been active for several years in the work of CCJ, joining the National Executive in 1970 and playing a leading role in the Hampstead Council. He was soon to take on the editorship of *Common Ground*, of which his book reviews particularly became a feature. The following year Mr Ronald Palin, who had served the Council for ten years as the other joint honorary secretary and whose wise counsel was widely respected, also retired. His place was taken by Rev. Philip Schofield, a United Reformed minister, who was also at the time co-secretary of the Rainbow dialogue group.

MOVES OF OFFICE

In 1977, CCJ had to vacate its pleasant offices in Cadogan Gardens and moved to the fourth floor, above a bank, of 48 Onslow Gardens in South Kensington. In 1983, there was a further move to the cramped attic rooms of the building. Lord Coggan, soon after taking on the chairmanship, climbed the six flights of stairs without any sign of breathlessness, but the stairs did discourage many visitors, and it was a long way down to take the rubbish when the Council's offices were moved, yet again, to Hampstead Synagogue's Community Hall, early in 1984.

THE CONTINUING WORK OF CCJ

In view of the financial difficulties and small size of the staff, it is amazing how much of the normal work of CCJ was continued and that new initiatives were taken. The financial appeal, which absorbed a lot of office time, and the changes to the constitution, meant that by 1979 CCJ was 'in a far better position to look ahead than could have been foreseen just a year before'.[10]

The educational work, which has always been a large part of CCJ's task, had continued. Peter Jennings and Leonard Goss addressed a wide variety of audiences. With the appointment of Anne Baring, the work increased rapidly. Soon a valuable audio-visual library was built up and CCJ commissioned its own audio-visual material. *Living Judaism*, produced for CCJ by Schapiro Programmes, has been a much-used set of slides with taped commentary, which gives an overview of Judaism. *In Good Faith* was an imaginative account of a building in Brick Lane, East London, which was originally a Huguenot chapel, then became a Methodist church, was then the Spitalfields Great Synagogue or 'Machzikei Hadath', and is now a mosque. Through the history of the building an introduction was given to the three faiths and to important issues in dialogue and community relations.

The 1970s was also a time of considerable public discussion about the pattern of religious education in local authority schools. Many felt that RE, moving from its inherited Christian basis, should become neutral and introduce pupils to the whole range of world religions. CCJ became an active member of the Religious Education Council and the Standing Conference on Interfaith Dialogue in Education, where these matters were discussed. Peter Jennings also helped to prepare a position paper for CCJ on this matter.

Simple publications continued to be produced. In 1978, for example, there were three additions to CCJ's occasional series: *Who were the Ioudaioi?* by Malcolm Lowe, *Israel, People of God – God, Destiny, Suffering* by Professor T.F. Torrance and *Jewish and Christian Festivals* by Joan Lawrence.

In addition to the revival of *Common Ground*, a *Newsletter* was introduced. This contained news of the activities of branches as well as of the activities of the central office. *Common Ground*, as a result, was free to become a journal with an appeal to a wider readership, as much of CCJ news was now in the *Newsletter*.

Local councils continued to grow during this period and staff members were regular in their visits to them.

The annual conference during this period moved from Cambridge, where accommodation had become too expensive. One conference was held at Spode House, but in 1979 the conference was held at Hengrave Hall, a large Tudor mansion near Bury St Edmunds. This has since become the favourite venue.

INTERNATIONAL LINKS

In 1976, a CCJ study tour to Israel was proposed. As, however, ICCJ had decided to hold an international conference in Jerusalem to mark the 30th anniversary of the Oxford conference, efforts were concentrated on arranging for a sizeable group from Britain to attend this. The Jerusalem conference, which lasted ten days, allowed participants quite a lot of time to get to know the country and its people. Delegates visited a reception centre for Jews who had recently arrived from the Soviet Union and they also went to Nes Ammim.

1977 saw a further increase in CCJ's involvement in international activities. An ICCJ youth conference was organised in Britain. Not surprisingly in view of the backgrounds of the staff, it was held in South Wales! The theme was 'Aspects of Violence'. Forty young people from six countries took part. In the same year, the international executive committee of ICCJ met in London and, later in the year, the ICCJ Colloquium was held at Southampton University, whither James Parkes' unique collection of books and pamphlets had recently been moved.

In 1980, in a historic moment, members of CCJ were received at a public audience by the Pope in Rome. A group of about 80 members took part in this visit to Rome. An interesting programme was arranged, including a visit to the Rome synagogue and to the Sisters of Sion. Bishop Gerald Mahon played a great part in the arrangements. At the audience, in a hall which holds thousands of people, Mr Sidney Corob, Sir Sigmund Sternberg, Rev. Peter Jennings and Mr Leonard Goss sat in the front row and the Pope spoke to each of them. Anne Baring, rather than herself speak to the Pope, presented to him Mrs M. Baumann of Finchley CCJ, who had at one time lived in Danzig and who was celebrating her 86th birthday. The Pope responded by saying, 'I greet you as a compatriot'.[11]

In 1980, an ICCJ youth conference was held in Israel and was attended by some young people from Britain. Discussions centred on the immense significance of the Holocaust and on the importance of Israel. The Arab-Jewish issue became all too topical, as during the conference the PLO planted a bomb at a nearby petrol station. Thirteen members of the public were injured, one of whom subsequently died.

Some members of the conference wished to make a statement

condemning the PLO's use of violence, whilst others felt that an Israeli incursion into southern Lebanon during the previous week must be mentioned as well. An Arab Christian member strongly believed that any statement would be interpreted as anti-Arab, and ultimately the conference accepted that viewpoint. Therefore no statement was made.[12]

ANTISEMITISM

As ever the Council kept a watchful eye on signs of antisemitism. A worrying aspect of this was the growth of antisemitism on university campuses. The good relations enjoyed by CCJ with university chaplains made it easier to combat this menace.[13]

Preparations for Oberammergau 1980 again led to discussion. An interesting initiative was taken by some clergy in Leeds. They wrote to a number of fellow clergy who might be considering taking a party asking them to think about the anti-Judaism of the play and suggesting that it would be more worthwhile and better value for money to take the group to the Holy Land.

ANTI-JUDAISM

By the mid-1970s, the teaching of Vatican II's *Nostra Aetate* was beginning to become better known in the Catholic Church. There was a determined attempt to purge Catholic liturgies and teaching of anti-Judaism. In this work the Sisters of Sion took a special lead. In 1979, the Central Committee of the World Council of Churches adopted *Guidelines on Dialogue Recommended to the Churches for Study and Action*, which gave an impetus to the approach of dialogue. One of the tasks of CCJ was to make known these international developments. Often church members are unaware of the changes taking place.

CCJ was also beginning to find new allies in the work. The Rainbow Group provided an opportunity for serious discussion between Jews and Christians, even on 'theological subjects'. This was set up largely on the initiative of Canon Peter Schneider, who had been the Archbishop in Jerusalem's special adviser and who on his return to England became consultant to the Archbishops on interfaith and Jewish affairs. Deeply committed to a new relationship between Jews and Christians, his early death was a tragic loss.

There was growing awareness of the horrors of the Holocaust. The TV series on the Holocaust, although much criticised for its 'soap opera' format, reached a very wide audience in the USA and Britain. At the same time, the opening of archives and public records in more and more European countries gave ever renewed evidence of the bestial acts that had been committed. Survivors too became more willing to tell of what had happened, lest a new generation should forget.[14]

ISRAEL

Concern for Israel continued, particularly at the time of the Yom Kippur War in 1973, when, for a short while, Israel was in real danger. Many Jews felt that the majority of Christians were silent during this crisis. The Executive, at its meeting on 6 December 1973, felt that any statement of the Council 'should stress the moral and religious, rather than the political, aspects of the issues involved and the need for justice and fairness in the eventual settlement, particularly in the solution of the problem of the Palestinian refugees'.[15]

In 1977, the Labour party in Israel was for the first time deprived of power and replaced by the right wing Likud government. Soon afterwards, however, President Sadat of Egypt made his historic journey to Jerusalem to address the Knesset – a move that was followed by the Camp David agreement. Hopes that a wider peace might follow were destined to disappointment and gradually public opinion in Britain moved against Israel, especially after the invasion of Lebanon.

CCJ, whilst still avoiding political comment, found it ever more necessary to try to explain to Christians the importance of Israel in Jewish self-understanding.[16] In 1980, the Executive once again protested about the executions taking place in Iran.[17]

INTO THE 1980s

By the end of the 1970s, CCJ had survived a difficult period but had laid the foundations for future growth. The deeper issues between

7. HH Pope John Paul II with Leonard Goss

8. (Seated l to r) Mr Sidney Corob, Lady Coggan, Lord Coggan,
(Standing l to r) Mrs Elizabeth Corob, Rev. Marcus Braybrooke, Mrs Rachel Hobin and
Mrs Mary Braybrooke

9. A Meeting of the Joint Presidents

10. (l to r) Rabbi Dr Albert Friedlander, Rev. Dr I. Levy, Cardinal Hume,
Sir Sigmund Sternberg and Canon Jim Richardson

Jews and Christians were coming to the surface and their importance was slowly being recognised by a wider public.

7

Expanding Horizons

In the Acts of the Apostles there are some well known 'we' passages. It is usually assumed that St Luke, the traditional author of the Acts of the Apostles, joined St Paul for some of his missionary journeys. Others think this was a literary device of the ancient world to give an air of verisimilitude. If this narrative now sometimes lapses into the first person, it is because I was appointed Executive Director in 1984 and took up the position in July of that year. I was, however, involved in various discussions from early that year and took part in the 1984 Hengrave Hall conference. Even so, I will try to avoid this reading like the self-justifying memoirs of a retired politician!

Whilst most of my work until that time had been as a parish clergyman, I had for many years also been involved in interfaith work, mainly as an officer of the World Congress of Faiths, although I joined CCJ in the early 1960s. Before ordination, I studied for a year in India, at Madras Christian College. My main field of study was Hinduism. I had, however, in 1977 spent three months at the Ecumenical Institute at Tantur, Jerusalem. I have still not mastered Hebrew, so at committee meetings the rabbis could carry on a second confidential discussion!

At the time of my appointment, CCJ had no house available. We had our own small 'retirement' cottage near Bath, so we decided to live there. This meant that my wife Mary could continue with her work as a social worker and magistrate. She would also still be near her friends, which was valuable if I was likely quite often to be away, although she was always ready to come to London for important CCJ events and never complained about getting back home in the early hours. For Mary had been in touch with CCJ, interfaith and peace work long before we met.

I was also asked if I would take the services, when I was available, at Christ Church in Bath. This church was built at the end of the eighteenth century as a proprietary chapel and was perhaps the first Church of England church not to charge pew rents. With a growing congregation, there was more to do than I had expected. This, with the travelling to London, contributed to my over-working, but I felt it important to be rooted in a community of faith. The more one meets with people of other faith traditions, the more one needs to be nourished in one's own.

FUTURE POLICY

At the June 1984 Executive meeting, there was considerable discussion of a policy paper. This set the priorities for the next few years. There were four headings: Education, Dialogue, Relationships and Finance.[1]

1. EDUCATION

Education was recognised to be a high priority. It was seen, however, that with CCJ's very limited staff, extensive school visiting was not the best use of time. Such visits are always worthwhile, but increasingly there are people in the locality with the necessary experience and expertise. Many rabbis devote a lot of time to talking to schools and to Christian groups. They also give generously of their time in showing parties round the local synagogue. Many local councils have made a big contribution to this work. Often it was the central office that made the original introduction. I heard by chance of one school which regularly had a talk from a local Jewish leader. The introduction had been made by the central office 16 years before and the work had continued ever since. A partial exception to this policy was the welcome given at central office to many young people who were taking part in one of the tours of 'Jewish London' which are arranged by the Board of Deputies.

Influencing Policy

More attention has been directed instead to educating the educators. CCJ's membership of the Religious Education Council and of the Standing Conference on Interfaith Dialogue in Education gave an opportunity to share in influencing policy. Members of local councils were often involved in the conferences responsible for drawing up syllabuses for RE. The introduction of GCSE also introduced changes to the syllabuses for Religious Studies. Some boards provided an opportunity to study Judaism. CCJ produced a short leaflet advising people of the options available. At a time too when managers were being given more say in how schools were run and about what was taught, a short paper for managers on the importance of RE was widely circulated.

When in 1988 changes relating to religious education were being introduced which seemed at first to threaten the position of children who were not Christian, CCJ voiced its concern and contacted the minister responsible and others involved in the debate.

Voluntary Aided Schools

An Education Advisory Committee was set up, which has done a variety of useful work. One of its first tasks was to discuss the role of voluntary aided religious schools. This was partly in response to the wish of some Muslims to set up aided Muslim schools – a development which some members of the public thought might be divisive. The key question, therefore, was whether religious schools need necessarily be divisive. Many would argue that those who are secure in their own faith are more sympathetic to the aspirations of those of other religions. The committee listened to heads of Jewish, Muslim (private), Roman Catholic and Anglican schools describe their policies.

Publications

The policy adopted on publications was rather similar. Continuing watchfulness lest textbooks should include prejudicial material (and CCJ's representations led to some books, such as *The Plantagenets*, being withdrawn or modified) was maintained. But by the late 1970s the study of world religions, for which CCJ had pressed since the sixties, had become a usual part of RE. As a result a large number of books about world religions, designed for use in schools or for teachers, were being published.

CCJ became increasingly involved in an advisory role to authors and publishers. This was more effective in reaching a wide audience than trying to produce too many of its own publications. Without easy channels of distribution, new publications would merely have added to those from a previous decade which already filled the office cupboards. It was also difficult for a voluntary body to match the quality and price of professional publications. CCJ also by keeping in touch with new publications was in a position to advise enquirers about the most suitable material for them to use.

Recently, with Sister Margaret Shepherd as Education Officer, a revitalised Education Committee has been planning a new series of popular booklets. One of the first will be a straightforward introduction to Judaism, called *A General Introduction to Judaism*, written by Rabbi Jeremy Rosen. A teacher's pack for non-specialist Religious Education (RE) staff, presenting the theme of 'Jesus the Jew' is being prepared. This will put Jesus in the context of a Jewish home and Jewish worship and culture. The pack will also link to Judaism today, including the rise of antisemitism, the Shoah and Israel. An introductory pack for RE teachers, centred on CCJ's educational work, is also being prepared. It is hoped, too, that a video version of CCJ's *Living Judaism* will soon be produced. The slide-tape format and indeed some of the pictures and commentary are now dated. The need for such an introductory video is considerable.

Common Ground

Canon Richardson quickly raised the question of how *Common Ground* could be made more attractive. Many local members felt it was rather academic and 'stuffy'. After various discussions at the Publications Committee, headed by Dr Elisabeth Maxwell with her abundant energy and enthusiasm, a new format has been developed, which makes the journal more attractive and easier to read. With the help of a strong editorial panel, the content has become more varied, although the high standard of contributions has been maintained. These improvements have been made possible through a generous gift, but it is now necessary to obtain advertisements so that *Common Ground* becomes self-financing.

The Media

In a similar way, CCJ sought to influence adult audiences through existing channels of communication. The religious press and the religious correspondents of the national newspapers and of the BBC were cultivated. Often their coverage was of issues in Christian–

Jewish relations rather than stories directly about CCJ. Yet in this way a widening circle of people has become aware of the importance of Christian–Jewish relations. The difficulty caused by missionary activity towards the Jews was covered in many national newspapers. There was a long correspondence in *The Times* in 1985, prompted by an article by Canon Dr Anthony Phillips, at the time chaplain of St John's College, Oxford, and consultant to the Archbishops on Jewish affairs, on 'Why the Jews must forgive'. A *Times* leader for Good Friday 1987, and several articles by Clifford Longley, the Religious Affairs correspondent, have been on the subject of Jewish–Christian relations. Fr Roger Clarke and Sr Margaret Shepherd and I have given a series of talks on the BBC World Service, and other members of staff have appeared on radio and television.

Press releases were regularly picked up in the religious press and the *Jewish Chronicle* now seldom appears without something about CCJ or related issues. Local radio too, especially in religious programmes where editors wanted to avoid a Christian monopoly, has given increasing attention to the work of local councils. Articles have also appeared in a wide variety of religious journals.

Educating Clergy and Rabbis

The main educational priority, however, was to help clergy and rabbis to become aware of the far-reaching changes taking place at a scholarly level in Christian–Jewish relations. A particular approach was made to those in theological colleges and seminaries. This was done partly by visits to colleges and contact with staff. Even more important, a young leadership programme has been developed. As a way of choosing young people to represent Britain at ICCJ Young Leadership conferences, for example in Israel or Canada, essay competitions have been held. Meetings for young people in Britain have also been arranged.

Leo Baeck Weekends

Of particular value have been the biennial conferences for ordinands held at Leo Baeck College. Participants have stayed in Jewish homes and shared the Sabbath evening meal there and then, on the next morning, have gone with their host family to a synagogue service. In addition they have attended lectures given by well-known members of the college, such as Rabbi Lionel Blue, Rabbi Julia Neuberger and the principal, Rabbi Jonathan Magonet, who is also active in the JCM, which arranges study weeks for young Jews, Christians and Muslims at Bendorf in Germany. These Leo Baeck weekends, which have allowed plenty of time for discussion, have been described as the biggest ecumenical gathering for Christians studying for the ministry! A wide range of denominations is represented.[2]

Conferences for Clergy

Before coming to CCJ, I had been working as Director of Training for Clergy and Laity in the Diocese of Bath and Wells. In the 1970s, most dioceses of the Church of England set up in-service training and refresher programmes for clergy. It seemed best to try to use these courses to reach the clergy. Events put on just by CCJ were likely only to attract those who were already interested. If however clergy were invited by their bishop, there was likely to be a higher attendance.

One of the first of these day conferences was held for the clergy of the London diocese and perhaps ten per cent of the clergy attended which, in so big a diocese, was a large number. The event was arranged jointly by the London Diocesan Council for Christian–Jewish Understanding and with the help of the Centre for the Study of Judaism and Jewish–Christian Relations, at the Selly Oak Colleges, Birmingham. This centre, through its 'Project Roots', has continued to arrange a series of clergy in-service conferences, with the support of CCJ. CCJ has also taken its own initiatives and in 1990, for example, arranged a two-day course for junior clergy in the diocese of Peterborough.

The Centre for the Study of Judaism and Jewish–Christian Relations

The Centre for the Study of Judaism and Jewish–Christian Relations, which was formally established in 1989, after several preparatory years, has been widely influential. It is led by Rabbi Dr Norman Solomon, who has been rabbi of Hampstead Synagogue and who is a much-sought-after teacher and a participant in international Jewish–Christian dialogue. The Centre's staff also includes

Rev. Allan Brockway, formerly on the staff of the World Council of Churches and Dr Margaret Brearley. Besides courses at Birmingham, members of staff have arranged conferences in many parts of the country and have spoken at numerous meetings.

Several other events arranged jointly by CCJ and the Centre for the Study of Judaism and Christian–Jewish Relations deserve a mention. With the full support of the Chief Rabbi, a day conference was arranged for Orthodox rabbis. Many of them had had little involvement in Christian–Jewish dialogue and were glad to learn of the developments.

'The Parting of the Ways'

Two important conferences entitled 'The Parting of the Ways' have been arranged. They were designed to equip those who attended to teach others about the issues in Jewish–Christian relations. At a Leo Baeck weekend for students, some of the theological college teachers had recognised the deficiencies of their own teaching, but did not know where to go for up-to-date material. In fact, of those who attended the conferences few came from colleges, and the attendance from overseas was suprisingly high, with participants from Israel, Sweden, Nigeria and the USA.

The first conference, held at Westhill College, Birmingham, in 1987, was based on the thesis that the split between Church and Synagogue did not take place at the time of Jesus, but some years later, following the fall of Jerusalem in 70 C.E. Many of the reasons for the split were social, economic and political. These reasons created the polemic, even if it was couched in theological terms. If today Christian and Jewish scholars can get behind the polemic of the first century, then a new approach to the theological issues may be possible. The second conference was held at York and also attracted a galaxy of well known speakers. This looked at developments in the mediaeval period. The conference included a service of reconciliation at Clifford's Tower, the scene in 1190 of the worst massacre of Jews in Britain. The original intention was to have a third conference on the modern period.

Clifford's Tower

It was at Clifford's Tower, York, that another major event was held in 1990 to mark the 800th anniversary of the tragic outburst of anti-

Jewish violence which occurred there. A seminar arranged by B'nai B'rith and CCJ began with a procession through the streets of York to Clifford's Tower. There a memorial gathering was conducted by the Archbishop of York, Dr Habgood, and Rabbi Dr Norman Solomon. Rabbi Walter Rothschild of Sinai Synagogue, Leeds, wrote of this occasion,

> Eight centuries further on, some things have changed – and some things have not ... A Rabbi, interested in Christianity, and an Archbishop, interested in Judaism, can stand together and recall a time when such companionship would have appeared unthinkable; a Cantor can sing, on this site where Jews have mourned, the Jewish prayers of mourning, and Christians can join in the 'Amen'. A brief service in the open air, in the middle of a modern, busy city – but a symbolic act of great significance.[3]

Concerts were arranged by the B'nai B'rith Musical Committee, led by Geraldine Auerbach. One of these was held in York Minster. Lectures were given. Two Synagogue services were held and special church services took place in the Minster and at Bar Convent. The climax of the Commemoration, in York Minster, was a joint gathering, entitled 'Expressions of Heritage and Hope', devised by Canon Geoffrey Hunter, with the approval of the Minster authorities and the officiating rabbis. The large congregation of Jews and Christians was welcomed by the Dean of York with the words, 'Now is the time for us to meet together in tearful recollection of March 1190 whose events we face in truth and penitence and to come together in courage and hope of God's better future'.[4]

Remembering for the Future

A conference of major importance was the one held to mark the 50th anniversary of Kristallnacht, when synagogues throughout Germany were destroyed on the 'night of broken glass'. Called 'Remembering for the Future: The Impact of the Holocaust and Genocide on Jews and Christians', this conference was arranged by Dr Elisabeth Maxwell and the Pergamon Press at Oxford in July 1988. It attracted nearly 400 scholars, many of whom had written papers in advance. In addition, a big public meeting was held in London and also a gathering of survivors. The thrust of the whole week was summed up by Dr Elisabeth Maxwell like this: 'Awareness of the Holocaust should become a measuring rod as we rethink our theologies and philosophies, as we carry out our professional and scientific tasks, and as we endeavour to recreate and perfect political relations.' A further aim was to see whether it was possible to develop 'an early warning system' by which to detect potentially genocidal movements.[5]

Ammerdown

Besides the courses specially arranged for clergy and rabbis, there have been increasing opportunities for interested adults to learn about both religions and about their relationships. The Ammerdown Conference Centre, near Bath, has regular courses and weekend conferences on the subject. The centre is run by an ecumenical community, many of whose members are Sisters of Sion. A frequent participant is Rabbi Lionel Blue, so well known for his regular broadcasts, and Fr Gordian Marshall, a Dominican priest who has been one of the Catholic leaders of the dialogue. Similar courses were also held at Spode House, Rugeley, before it closed.

Courses and Lectures

The Open University's course on 'The Religious Quest', with good material on all world religions, reached a wide audience. There have been many other educational programmes on television about Judaism and Jewish–Christian relations, for example Abba Eban's monumental series *Heritage: Civilization and the Jews*, Claude Lanzmann's disturbing film *Shoah* and the challenging programme *Shadow on the Cross*.

The extra-mural departments of several universities, such as London, Birmingham, Bristol, Newcastle and others, have arranged courses on the subject. At Manchester, there is now a regular programme of what are called the Sherman Lectures. Those given by Emil Fackenheim, Professor at Toronto and the author of many books on the Holocaust, and by Geoffrey Wigoder of the Hebrew University, who is an active member of the Jerusalem Rainbow Group, have been published.[6] Programmes have also been arranged at Southampton under the auspices of the Parkes Library, and there have been meetings at many churches, for example at St James', Piccadilly and St Martin-in-the-Fields.

Whilst CCJ is often consulted for its advice and is always glad to help in publicizing programmes, it is a sign of the importance now given to the subject that so many people are taking initiatives in this field. Often, they are individual members of CCJ. The programmes of CCJ, both locally and nationally, make a major contribution to the educational work. Local councils in more than 40 centres arrange regular programmes. The Waley Cohen lecture, the annual Hengrave Hall Conference, the annual conference of the Standing Conference of Local Councils, now hosted each year by a different local council, and other meetings are regular events.

Sometimes CCJ has arranged special meetings when an interesting speaker from abroad is in London. For example, a public discussion between Dr Pinchas Lapide, an Orthodox Jew who wrote a book about the resurrection of Jesus, Sr Mary Kelly of the Sisters of Sion and Rabbi Dr Norman Solomon was held in 1986 at the Friends' Meeting House in Euston Road, London.

Kristallnacht

A particularly important meeting was that held to mark the 50th anniversary of Kristallnacht on 9 November 1988. The Archbishop of Canterbury, Dr Robert Runcie, acknowledged that Kristallnacht had its origins deep in the history of Christian Europe. 'Without centuries of Christian antisemitism, Hitler's passionate hatred would never have been so fervently echoed ... Without the poisoning of Christian minds through centuries, the holocaust is unthinkable.' Dr Runcie recognised too that 'We cannot say, "We did not know". We did – and stood by'.[7] Cardinal Hume, Archbishop of Westminster, deplored the tendency of some to try to minimise the Shoah. He affirmed that 'there has to be unequivocal recognition of the fact that God chose in a unique way the Jewish people as a channel for the revelation of Himself and of His saving plan for humankind'.[8] The Chief Rabbi, Lord Jakobovits, voiced the hope that 'from the darkness, from the night unmatched in human history, may we see the radiance of a new light, a new peace, a new brotherhood that will never again allow humans to grieve for inhumanity, and that will hail the triumph of rebuilding and rebirth'.[9]

More Books

The increasing public interest and awareness are reflected in the growing number of publications, both about Judaism and about Jewish–Christian relations. SCM Press, for example, which has a long history of publishing important works of Christian theology, has not only published several books by Christians on Jewish issues, but has recently published several books by Jewish scholars. Christian theology, especially biblical studies, is showing greater sensitivity to Jewish study, whilst more Jews than at any previous period of history are writing about Jesus and about other Christian topics.

DIALOGUE

Educational work quickly turns into dialogue. Just as educational work in this field is rapidly growing and is no longer the preserve of CCJ, although much of it is stimulated and coordinated by the Council, so too dialogue takes place at many levels and at many venues. Indeed the role of the Council is to encourage people to meet in a friendly atmosphere and to talk. Once the dialogue begins, CCJ can take a step back, ready to offer support when required.

In the 1984 policy memorandum, dialogue was acknowledged as 'the vehicle to stimulate mutual understanding and respect between the adherents of different faiths'. It was agreed that CCJ should encourage dialogue between Jews and Christians on a variety of subjects and 'not refrain from theological discussions'. This was an important phrase, since the Chief Rabbi (as he said in his Lambeth lecture), along with other Orthodox Jewish leaders, was reluctant to engage in theological discussion. Whilst respecting this position, CCJ was no longer prepared to be bound by it. Otherwise much of the more creative dialogue would take place outside the auspices of CCJ. To avoid the suggestion of 'indifferentism' – an old bogy – the memorandum spoke of awareness of 'the differences that exist between Jewish and Christian communities'.

The memorandum also agreed to 'examine the relationship between the State of Israel and British Jewry and its significance for Christian–Jewish dialogue'. Whilst still aware that CCJ was not a political organisation – although some members of the Executive thought it was in danger of becoming so – the Executive realised that Israel must be on the agenda of dialogue. For some time, in CCJ circles, the topic had been avoided, although after the Lebanon invasion Israel was regularly in the news headlines. It was evidently artificial to avoid the question of Israel and to avoid theology. To be serious, CCJ had to grapple with the burning issues of the day, hoping that the trust already built up would be sufficient to allow frank discussion of differences. Another concern mentioned, reflecting Lord Coggan's and Sir Sigmund Sternberg's support for Keston College, was 'the plight of Jews and Christians behind the Iron Curtain and in other countries where the free expression of religion is suppressed'.[10]

Opportunities for Dialogue

An account of the many occasions for dialogue could begin with the discussions in someone's sitting room as a local committee meets to plan its programme. Perhaps we should begin at the top as the joint presidents meet in an elegant drawing room at Lambeth Palace. Quite likely, the same subjects will be discussed in both places: Israel, moral issues, combating prejudice, or preparing for the next festival.

The Joint Presidents

Throughout CCJ's history, the joint presidents, the acknowledged religious leaders in Britain, have been supportive of the Council. All the Archbishops of Canterbury have given it their full backing. Yet, although the leaders had quite often appeared on the same platform, there seems until recently to have been only limited informal discussion and contact. For some time, the Chief Rabbi had wished for closer relationships. This was mentioned to me by Mr Moshe Davis, who had been on the Chief Rabbi's staff, and who had made in his own quiet way an invaluable contribution to Christian–Jewish relations. The Archbishop kindly agreed to host a private meeting of the joint presidents and all accepted his invitation. Then, at the last moment, the funeral of the Duchess of Windsor was arranged at the same time as the meeting had been planned to begin. With memories of the Abdication in the air, the Archbishop had to be seen to be at her funeral service, at which he gave the blessing. The meeting was rearranged for December 1986. The Archbishop's chaplain was quite apprehensive and thought the atmosphere would be icy (partly because of difficulties about Israel). In fact, the mood was quite the reverse and when we tentatively suggested that there should be a similar meeting in two years' time, it was agreed to make it an annual event. Cardinal Hume had not been able to attend the first meeting because of illness – but this was a genuine illness, not like the 'diplomatic indisposition' of one of his predecessors! The Cardinal was at the next meeting and has been an enthusiastic participant.

The meetings are private and no press release is issued. They have, however, allowed the leaders to compare their reactions to topics of the day, for example the moral and religious response to Aids, the problems of the inner cities, educational changes and events in Israel and the Middle East – during much of this time Terry Waite has been held hostage.

The meetings have perhaps gained added significance from the increasingly prominent role that the Chief Rabbi and Jewish leaders have played in British public life in the 1980s. Knighted in 1981, Dr Jakobovits was made a life peer in 1988. Although this was a personal honour, it was seen by many as a broadening of the acknowledged religious leadership of the nation to include others than Christians. Many feel ambivalent about the role of bishops in the House of Lords and think that leaders of other Churches and faith communities should also have a seat there. It has to be seen whether Lord Jakobovits' peerage is a precedent. The Archbishop has also gone out of his way to acknowledge the Chief Rabbi's distinguished contribution to national life and in a historic ceremony granted him an honorary Lambeth doctorate.

Official discussions between representatives of the Jewish world and Christian Churches have become more regular in recent years. As a voluntary body, CCJ has no direct relationship to them, but members are often participants and the Council has brought the fruits of these meetings to a wider public. Further reference will be made to such official dialogue in the chapter on International Involvements.[11]

The Rainbow Group

There are a growing number of informal dialogue groups. The Rainbow Group was established in 1976, at a meeting held in the Jerusalem Chamber of Westminster Abbey. Under the co-chairmanship of Rev. Dr Edward Carpenter and Rabbi Hugo Gryn, of the West London Synagogue, it has met regularly to hear and discuss a paper. Each year also an annual meeting, open to a wider public, has been arranged. Recently, the attendance has become rather variable so that something of the earlier coherence of the group has been lost. In 1991, therefore, it was decided to disband the group. A wide range of topics has been covered, including, recently, 'Penitential Thought in Judaism and Christianity', 'Towards a Christian Agenda for Jews', and 'Dialogue and the Women's Movement'.

Manor House Group

A smaller group which has been quite influential is the Manor House Group. This arose originally from a meeting of the Reform Rabbis at which Bishop Konstant, now Catholic Bishop of Leeds, and I were asked to speak. There was a feeling that much Jewish–Christian meeting was superficial. With the support of Lord Blanch, former Archbishop of York, and thanks in large measure to the enthusiasm of Rabbi Tony Bayfield, a small group of Christians (mainly Anglican) and Jews (mainly Reform) agreed to meet three times a year – one of these meetings being residential at the Quakers' conference centre at Charney Bassett. Again, these meetings are private, but a number of participants, such as the Bishop of Oxford, Richard Harries, Rabbi Julia Neuberger, Dr Albert Friedlander, Dr Hyam Maccoby, Rabbi Dr Norman Solomon, Rev. Dr John Bowden, Rev. Dr Alan Race and others, by their books or radio or television appearances, have shared something of the discussions with a wider public.

The Black-led Churches

A particularly interesting development was the establishment of a small group of rabbis, and clergy, some of whom were members of the black-led churches. The latter had often felt rather excluded from ecumenical activities. They soon found a real affinity to their Jewish colleagues and the white clergy almost felt *de trop*. A shared interest was the place of religious minorities in an increasingly secular society. As a result of this contact, leaders of the black-led churches have begun to play their part in CCJ's activities.

RELATIONSHIPS

This was the third heading of the memorandum. It was recognised that CCJ's influence could only be extended by contact with many related bodies, such as the British Council of Churches, the Free Church Federal Council, the various denominational headquarters, the Board of Deputies and various Synagogue councils. In each community too there were a variety of bodies with whom it was important to liaise, for example about Israel or about the position of believers in the Soviet Union, or with welfare organisations. The attempt to relate to a wide range of educational bodies has already been mentioned.

Of particular interest was the note that CCJ should 'be aware of interfaith activity in a wider context including relations with ethnic and religious minorities'.[12] My own background had been in wider interfaith work, especially as an officer of the World Congress of Faiths. In the early 1980s, there was little overlap between those committed to Christian–Jewish dialogue and those concerned for interfaith dialogue. Christians who had come to recognise that God's covenant with Israel is still valid, and that therefore God's saving love is not confined to Christians, had not made the step of seeing that the same love might be known through all the religions of the world. Those engaged in wider dialogue were often unaware of the specific issues in Christian–Jewish dialogue.

The Interfaith Network

CCJ, which had always been committed to the struggle against all discrimination, was therefore from the beginning a supporter of the suggestion of forming an Interfaith Network for the UK. The initiator was Brian Pearce, who is now a member of the CCJ Executive. Sir Sigmund Sternberg gave generous backing and Rabbi Hugo Gryn became a co-chairperson. The Network links together representatives of the various religious communities in Britain, national interfaith organisations and local interfaith groups.

Muslims

Although there has been the suggestion that CCJ should become CCJM – the Council of Christians, Jews and Muslims – this has not commanded much support. Muslims have been invited to speak at the Hengrave Conference and to join in some other discussions. It has been felt that there is still a large and specific agenda for Christians and Jews to tackle together. There are separate but important agendas for Jews and Muslims and for Christians and Muslims. Whilst on occasion, it is good for all three to meet together, it has seemed better to encourage various patterns of dialogue.

Other Links

CCJ has sought to maintain good relations with other interfaith bodies, such as the World Congress of Faiths. Its concern for peace has also been shared with the World Conference on Religion and Peace and the United Nations Association Religious Advisory Committee, of which Dr Edward Carpenter has been chairperson for many years.

The difficulty with so small a staff has been to keep up with all these related organisations and to attend the necessary meetings – but nearly always some subject is of direct relevance to the concerns of the Council and, of course, attendance at these meetings helps the Council to get better known. Organisations are often personified by their representatives.

Internal Relationships

The memorandum also spoke of internal relationships within CCJ. Of special importance was the building of a closer relationship with all local councils. We shall return to this subject in the chapter on Local Councils.[11]

Sub-committees

The importance of amicable relations between officers and staff was also stressed. To encourage this, periodic officers/staff meetings were held, usually in the comfort of the Mayfair office of Mr Sidney Corob, with his well-known hospitality. The aim, not entirely achieved, was to avoid this being just a business/standing committee, so that the discussion could be more informal and relaxed and range over key topics in Christian–Jewish relations.

A recent development of great significance has been the establishment of a chairman's advisory panel, which the chairman can call together when there is a specific matter of importance to discuss. Membership includes Rev. David Craig, of the BBC World Service, Judge Israel Finestein, Sir Claus Moser, Mr Michael Latham, MP, Lord Weidenfeld, Canon Anthony Harvey, Mr Sidney Corob, Dr Elisabeth Maxwell and Rabbi Dr Norman Solomon, with Canon Richardson, now Executive Director, in attendance.

Equally significant is the development of advisory committees. These have involved a far wider range of people in the activities of CCJ and allowed more work to be undertaken. The Education Advisory Committee and the Publications Committee have already been mentioned. The Missionary Monitoring Committee, which is chaired by Fr Gordian Marshall, came into being at a time when the 'Jews for Jesus' movement seemed likely to cause real difficulties between the Jewish community and the Churches. It has continued patient, sometimes painful, discussions about the theological issues raised by missionary activity. The committee's importance is likely to be highlighted during the Decade of Evangelism.

The Israel Advisory Committee has recently been reconstituted. Its task is to study the situation in Israel 'within a wide context, having in mind contemporary problems and attitudes', to educate and inform Christians about Israel and to acquaint the Jewish community with Christian perspectives, to monitor the media, to produce briefing material, to encourage and promote dialogue about Israel with religious leaders and groups and 'to explore theologically the concepts of Land and Covenant within Judaism and Christianity'.[13]

Staff

The importance of harmonious relations amongst all members of staff was also stressed in the memorandum. This should perhaps have been self-evident in an organisation devoted to building up good relations between peoples – but neither charities nor religious groups can always escape personal tensions. The non-smoker, however religious, may object to his colleague's cigar smoke! More seriously, in a small office, members of staff have to cover for each other. Whilst people may have special responsibilities, education cannot just stop for two weeks, whilst the education officer is leading a tour to Israel or is on holiday. Most members of staff have to help with the typing and with phone calls. It is no easier to apply all the normal principles of management and business technique to a small charitable organisation than it is to the National Health Service. An enquiry may take an hour or so to deal with, but there may be no tangible reward – not even a subscription to CCJ.

During my time at CCJ, I was very grateful for the loyalty and cooperation of all the staff. The illness and subsequent death of Len Goss was a real blow. His widow, Mildred, however, has continued as general secretary, with multitudinous tasks and with an unrivalled knowledge of CCJ's members. Len Goss's place was taken by Paul Mendel, who came to CCJ with wide experience of the business world and of communal work. He was originally appointed as Assistant Director, but is now Deputy Director. Much of his first year was spent obtaining funds for a computer system from the Greater London Council, which was in its death throes, and then of installing it. Despite some mixed feelings at first among the staff, the computer has transformed the amount of work of which the office is capable and been an important tool in extending its influence. Increasingly, Paul has taken on a great weight of administration, whilst keeping abreast of all the issues with which the Council deals. His dedication has helped to give continuity to the varied work of CCJ.

Rev. Graham Jenkins, generously shared with me his deep knowledge of the subject. His place was taken by Fr Roger Clarke, a Dominican priest. Graham had demonstrated the importance of having on the staff a Catholic who was *au fait* with the subject and who knew the personalities in the Catholic Church. Roger, a good scholar, had spent a year studying at Leo Baeck College, before joining CCJ; the Dominican Order generously made him available for this work. However, after two years he left to become Prior of the Dominican house at Edinburgh.

Roger Clarke's place was taken by Sister Margaret Shepherd, a Sister of Sion. The Sisters of Sion's primary work is to foster good relations between Christians and Jews. Margaret had her secondary education at a school run by the Sisters. After completing her teacher's training, she herself became a Sister of Sion. She taught English for several years, but then wanted to concentrate on the Order's primary work. She spent three years studying rabbinics at Leo Baeck College. Then, for nine years, before she joined the staff of CCJ, she worked at the Order's Study Centre for Christian–Jewish relations in West London.

Acknowledgement needs also to be made of the Finance Officers, David Loftus and subsequently Mrs Barbara Hall. Both have given generously of their time and energy and have been willing to be involved in other aspects of the Council's work.

Because of health problems, my time as Executive Director was cut short and I retired at the end of 1987.

Canon Richardson

The following year, the Council was fortunate to attract to the post Canon Jim Richardson. At the time, he was Vicar of Leeds, one of the most senior parochial appointments in the Church of England. He was active in the civic life of the city, which has a large Jewish population, and he was chairman of Leeds CCJ. He was already well known as a broadcaster and writer in the area. He knows Israel well. In 1985 and 1987 he led the BBC Radio Leeds Listeners' Pilgrimage to the Holy Land, and has led many other parties to it and to neighbouring countries. Richardson was born in Exeter in 1942, but brought up mainly in London. After a short spell in industry when he left school, he went to Hull University to read Law and Political Studies. This was followed by a year's post-graduate teacher training course at Sheffield. After two years' teaching, Richardson sought ordination and went to Cuddesdon Theological College, near Oxford. He worked as a curate at St Peter's Collegiate Church, Wolverhampton and then moved to Stoke-on-Trent. In 1975, he was appointed Rector of Nantwich and moved to Leeds in 1982.

With imagination and energy, Canon Richardson has made clear CCJ's stand on key issues and has helped CCJ to tackle a number of organisational problems, not least the revision of the constitution and the relations to local councils. He has helped to give the organisation a higher profile.

Chairman

In 1986, Lord Coggan retired as chairman. With his ready wit, he had made friends wherever he went. His firm and decisive chairmanship enabled decisions to be made which fostered the growth of the Council. His gift of encouragement inspired a renewed confidence and his personal reputation enhanced the standing of the Council.

He was followed by Rev. Dr Edward Carpenter, who had just retired as Dean of Westminster Abbey. Dr Carpenter has had a lifetime of involvement in interfaith, Christian–Jewish and peace work. He has brought a wealth of experience to the Council and has been generous in the time he has given to it. His friendly, eirenic manner has eased the way through some of the contentious issues with which the Council is regularly concerned.

Vice-Chairmen

Throughout the period Mr Sidney Corob has been an enthusiastic and generous vice-chairman. He has seen in CCJ 'a bastion of defence against antisemitism'. He has also encouraged CCJ both in its educational work and in its efforts to help Christians appreciate Jewish concern for Israel. With many interests in Israel, Mr Corob is Chairman of the British Technion Society. He is also active in various welfare groups in Britain, including the Central Council for Jewish Social Service and VOCAL, and in supporting the work of the Little Sisters of the Poor.

In the early 1980s, the other joint vice-chairman was Rev. Dr Arthur Chadwick of the United Reformed Church. He was chairman, for many years, of Manchester CCJ and then took a leading part in the work of the Standing Conference of Local Councils, before becoming the national vice-chairman. He was succeeded by Bishop Gerald Mahon, Roman Catholic Bishop of West London. Gerald Mahon worked for some years in Africa and served at that time on the Vatican Secretariat Committee for Non-Christians. He is now a member of the International Catholic–Jewish Liaison Committee.

Secretaries

Throughout the 1980s, Harry Levy, whose active interest in CCJ began with the establishment of the Hampstead Council in 1947, continued as one of the honorary secretaries. In 1981, Rev. Michael Porteus, an Anglican, became the Christian joint honorary secretary. At the time he was Vicar of St Jude's in Hampstead

Garden Suburb, where more of his parishoners were Jews than Christians! He did much to build up good relations in the area. He was succeeded by Rev. Eric Allen, a United Reformed minister, who has had many years' experience of Christian–Jewish dialogue, particularly as a member of the World Council of Churches' Consultation on the Church and the Jewish People. Eric is now Moderator of the Mersey Province of the United Reformed Church, but regularly attends London meetings and is a witness to the fact that CCJ is a national organisation.

Treasurers

Sir Sigmund Sternberg has continued as one of the honorary treasurers throughout the 1980s. He has combined this work with the chairmanship of the Executive of the International Council of Christians and Jews and with involvement in many other Christian–Jewish and interfaith organizations. To mention but a few, Sir Sigmund is Co-Chairman of Keston College, a Governor of the Hebrew University, a Trustee of the Sternberg Centre for Judaism and a Judge of the Templeton Foundation. He is active also in a host of charitable and welfare causes, such as VOCAL and CRUSE.

For a time Sir Julian Hodge was the Christian honorary treasurer. He was followed by Lady Avon, the widow of Anthony Eden, and her place was taken by Sir Reginald Pullen, who had been Chapter Clerk, Receiver General and Registrar of Westminster Abbey.

IMAGE AND FINANCE

The fourth item of the memorandum was finance. Its authors were confident that if adequate publicity were given to the programme, and a suitable programme was built up, then this would attract the desired financial support. Indeed in an unguarded moment, the treasurer said that without a sizeable deficit, one could not mount a large appeal! This may be compared with the position in the early 1970s, where staff and programme were cut back to keep within the available budget.

Income has indeed increased. This increase was needed, in part, in order to purchase a house for the director, as, if the Council wants a Christian clergyman for that post, he is likely to need to have a house provided. A modern four-bedroomed house on the edge of Northampton was found and Canon ·Richardson moved there in September 1988. The distance from the office is about 70 miles, but the M1 is close both to the house and the office. The cost of property nearer to London was prohibitive. The purchase itself was made possible largely by Mr Corob's generosity and fund-raising efforts.

More money has also been required to increase the activities of the Council, and there is also an urgent need to increase the number of members of staff and secretarial help. A million pounds appeal has been launched which has met with a good initial response. Earlier, a dinner given by the Speaker of the House of Commons raised a good sum, and a chairman's appeal by Lord Coggan yielded over £11,000.

Image and finance partly belong together. Whereas dialogue should not have any hidden motives, there are usually several motives for arranging major events. They have a symbolic value in expressing the new partnership of Jews and Christians; at the same time they are media events which raise the Council's image and thereby donations to the cause are encouraged.

Several major events have been of a commemorative nature. Some have already been mentioned, including the big gathering held at the Friends' Meeting House on the 50th anniversary of Kristallnacht, and the commemorative event at Clifford's Tower, 800 years after the massacre of the Jews of York.

The Royal Reception

The Royal Reception graciously given by Her Majesty the Queen, as Patron of the Council, at St James's Palace in 1989 was a happy occasion. She spoke to a number of members. A wide spectrum of the Council's membership was present, including representatives of most local councils. The event enhanced the Council's profile and was the basis for some subsequent fund-raising.

Kaddish for Terezim

In 1986, the world première of Ronald Senator's *Kaddish for Terezim*, a musical work commemorating the victims of the Shoah, was held in Canterbury Cathedral. The text, prepared by Rabbi Dr

CHILDREN OF ONE GOD

Albert Friedlander, included some of the poems and diaries written by the children of Terezin concentration camp. 'The real heart of the requiem', writes Albert Friedlander, 'remains in my life – it is a Kaddish, a prayer of remembrance for the children, all of whom are to go on living through us'.[14]

How Canterbury came to be chosen as the venue is worth recording. Some time earlier I was staying at the Ecumenical Institute at Tantur, near Jerusalem. Victor de Waal, then Dean of Canterbury, was also a visitor there. One morning a small group of us visited the School of Peace at Neve Shalom. Victor and I started talking and I mentioned that I had recently been to New York where, in the Cathedral of St John the Divine, there is a statue in memory of the victims of the Holocaust. Victor said he would like something similar at Canterbury, but wished it could be a living reminder. Soon after I got back to Britain, Geraldine Auerbach of B'nai B'rith came to see me to discuss a possible venue for *Kaddish for Terezim*. The suggestion of Canterbury was taken up and the cathedral authorities readily agreed. The evening, as Albert Friedlander says, was a great experience and 'meant a great deal to the Jews and Christians who heard it'.[15] It was a fitting tribute to the victims and a symbol of the new relationship of Jews and Christians.

The Fiftieth Anniversary

Now plans are in hand to mark the Fiftieth Anniversary of the Council. A committee, headed by Mr Paul Winner, has suggested setting up a Media Awards Programme for outstanding contributions to promoting racial tolerance. There would be many different categories for television, radio and various types of newspapers and journals. Another suggestion is that CCJ should establish a network of retail shops, similar to those run by Save the Children Fund and Oxfam. It is also hoped to arrange a programme of special events, including a tour of cathedrals, at which concerts and recitals would be given by well known musicians. Local councils are also being encouraged to arrange commemorative events.

A DEVELOPING PROGRAMME

It would be misleading to constrain the work of CCJ within the terms of one memorandum, although it has provided a useful framework for an account of recent activities. New initiatives are constantly being undertaken, whilst old issues recur. Many of these will be taken up in a subsequent chapter, when the subjects which are central to the Council's work are discussed. In the early 1980s, the question of Christian missionary activity, brought to the fore by the work of 'Jews for Jesus', attracted publicity. CCJ issued a statement distancing itself from aggressive missionary activity and the targeting of Jews. As the statement had the approval of the joint presidents, the main Churches' support for this position was implied.[16]

Later, attitudes to Israel, always a controversial topic, brought CCJ into dispute with some other Christian organisations, notably Christian Aid and the British Council of Churches. CCJ was critical both of a Christian Aid video, *The Much Promised Land*, which was thought only to put the Palestinian case, and also of the report *Impressions of Intifada*, produced by a British Council of Churches delegation which visited 'Israel and the Occupied territories' for a week in March 1989.[17] Rev. Dr Harry Levy prepared a detailed critique of the paper. In June 1990, a special meeting of the Executive was held, devoted to these issues. The Rt Rev. John Dennis, the Bishop of St Edmundsbury and Ipswich, who had been a member of the delegation, spoke to the meeting and responded to criticisms of the report *Impressions of Intifada*.[18] Earlier, in an open letter to the Archbishop, the chairman, Dr Edward Carpenter, made clear CCJ's position. CCJ had to take note of the importance of Israel to British Jewry, although, as a charity, it was not in a position to make political comments. Its task was to help the growth of mutual understanding and sympathy.[19]

In trying to do this, shortly before the start of the Intifada, CCJ had produced a simple leaflet for pilgrims, entitled *Pray for the Peace of Jerusalem*. This gave a very short background account of the history and situation in Israel, so that visitors would be more sympathetic to all involved in the tensions and less quick to judge. It was widely distributed through several companies which arrange pilgrimages.

An even more important new initiative was a joint Jewish–Christian study tour to Israel in the summer of 1990, led by Canon Richardson, Mr Paul Mendel and Rev. Malcolm Weisman. For some it was a first visit, so there were stops at the usual Christian holy sites. But there was also a chance to meet with several leaders of the Jewish and Arab communities. A visit to the Mayor of Bethlehem was especially memorable. The party also greeted the Sabbath at the Western wall and shared in a Sabbath meal in the old city of Jerusalem. There were visits to several synagogues. In Jerusalem, Canon Richardson laid a wreath, on behalf of CCJ, at Yad Vashem, the memorial to the victims of the Holocaust. At the end of the tour, the party joined in a tree-planting ceremony to inaugurate the CCJ Grove of Trees.

A visit to Israel of a group of young adults, led by Sister Margaret Shepherd, which took place earlier in 1990, was also an important educational initiative. One participant, Rev. Andrew Teal, wrote that, 'the quality of the week – its fairness to all sides and its faithfulness to claim and counterclaim: to conflicting ideologies and more significantly, conflicting tragedies, was profoundly and deeply affecting'.[20]

It is hoped that such tours will become regular features of CCJ's programme. Plans are in hand for another Christian–Jewish tour and for further study tours for young adults. A new initiative was a church leaders' tour, offering structured study, meetings and visits. It was arranged with the help of the Melitz Centre for Christian Encounter with Israel, which is headed by Dr Daniel Rossing.

Most recently, the recurrence of antisemitism in many parts of Europe and in Britain has caused new worries. The dramatic events of 1990 in Eastern Europe have been accompanied by a resurgence of antisemitism. This was a major concern voiced to the Pope when a CCJ delegation to Rome, in November 1990, was granted a private audience with His Holiness. In Britain, several Jewish cemeteries have been desecrated and there is some increase in anti-semitism, both on the far Left and amongst some Muslim extremists, as well as on the extreme Right. Criticism of Israel sometimes seems to show veiled antisemitism and some of the comments during discussions about the Nazi War Crimes Bill were also felt to reflect this.

CCJ has been outspoken in warning of these dangers and alerting the Churches to them. Considerable publicity was given to the summer editorial in *Manna*, which was headed 'Still the Church stays silent'. In fact, the World Council of Churches has now issued a statement denouncing antisemitism and the Pope in his reply to the CCJ delegation has spoken out against this evil, as have the leaders of British Churches.[21]

CCJ, true to its remit, continues to warn of the evil of anti-semitism and seeks by education to eradicate it. It is sad that, after all that has been achieved, the task is still as urgent today as it was when CCJ was formed 50 years ago.

8

Local Councils

When CCJ was formed, there were already some Jewish–Christian friendship groups in a few cities. Very quickly efforts were made to support such initiatives and to encourage the formation of local councils. At the meeting of the Executive on 5 November 1942, Simpson reported that a Joint Committee of Jews and Christians existed in Oxford. He was also in touch with people in Newcastle-upon-Tyne and Letchworth. A Council of Christians and Jews in Birmingham was formed in the spring of 1943. Soon mention was made of Jewish–Christian committees in Cambridge, Plymouth, Leeds, Manchester, Southgate, Sunderland, Darlington, Southport, East and West Ham, Brighton and Hove, North-West London, Liverpool, Leicester, Pontypool, Cardiff and St Albans.[1] Simpson travelled extensively, especially when one remembers the difficulty of war-time travel.

Soon, however, the question became insistent of how local councils could play a full part in the work of the national CCJ. The answer has required a prolonged struggle to turn CCJ into a democratic body. It is to be hoped that the changes made to the constitution at the 1990 annual general meeting have brought this struggle to a successful conclusion.

In this chapter, we shall look first at the developing and often uneasy relationship of local councils to the national Council. We shall then give a picture of the life of some local councils at different periods of CCJ's history and also, by way of illustration, recall the history of a few councils.

RELATIONS WITH THE CENTRE

In 1947, on 17 June, a meeting of national and local councils was held at Bloomsbury House. This was well attended. Birmingham, Newcastle, Manchester, Cardiff, Leicester, Leeds, Sunderland and

South Shields were represented. Much of the meeting was devoted to a thorough discussion of the extent of antisemitism and to ways of combating it. The relationship of local councils to the national Council was also discussed.[2]

Following the meeting, representatives of local councils began to be asked to the annual meeting. Regular efforts were also made to keep in touch with local councils. Simpson visited many of them and became a well-known friend. Further, not all the members of the national executive were from London.

Some attempts were made to convene a national meeting of representatives, but for several years they came to nothing, as did the hopes of appointing a field officer. There was a feeling, mentioned several times in minutes and correspondence, that relationships with local councils had not been fully worked out. This was a problem not confined to CCJ, but common to organisations of this type.

Conference of Local Council Representatives

In 1962, a Conference of Local Council Representatives was held at the Ivanhoe Hotel in London. Welcoming the participants, Carl Witton-Davies said that the Executive was regularly informed of the activities of local councils. The first evening was devoted to reports of the local councils' activities. On the second morning, there was discussion about the possibility of making 'Brotherhood Week', which was observed in Manchester, into a national event. It was also agreed to reintroduce CCJ summer schools, which had been discontinued because of lack of support. There was also a report on plans for an international Christian–Jewish youth conference.

A report, prepared for the meeting, shows that local councils had different financial relationships with the national office. Some collected the subscriptions of associate members and passed half to the national office. Other councils kept all the money, although some made occasional donations to the headquarters, whilst other councils made an extra charge to those members who wished to receive *Common Ground* and other mailings from the central office. From the national point of view the situation was felt to be unsatisfactory. It was the result of 'the high degree of autonomy of the local councils, most of which have come into being on local initiative,

The Standing Conference of Local Councils

The introduction of regular conferences for representatives of local councils failed to allay the feeling that local councils were not fully involved in the work of CCJ. This was expressed at a meeting of local representatives held in January 1969. Dr I. Levy put forward the Hampstead council's view that the national Executive had become a 'self-perpetuating body with little or no connection with people working in the field. They would like to see it develop into a more representative and democratic body.' They also wanted a working committee to strengthen local councils. 'Jews and Christians should work together and think together more in relation to such common social problems as race relations, family life today, drugs, the influence of the media and other contemporary issues.' Dr Levy then proposed the formation of a 'National Representative Council', composed of two members of each local council, which would strengthen the links between the national Executive and local councils.[4]

After a further meeting of representatives in July, the Standing Conference of Local Councils met for the first time on 29 October 1969. It was made clear that its role was advisory. It was suggested that the chairman of the Standing Conference should become an *ex officio* member of the Executive and this was agreed to by the Executive. The Standing Conference of Local Councils, which is now known as the Association of Local Branches, has facilitated communication in both directions.

Even so, the problem of involvement was not solved. In 1970, for example, Mrs Zoe Young, the organising secretary of Manchester CCJ, who had recently become the first chairman of the Standing Conference of Local Councils, wrote to Simpson: 'I don't feel there is sufficient cooperation yet and I would like to see the Local Councils playing a more active part in the overall affairs of the Council.'[5] There was a particular difficulty over a questionnaire that she had sent out to local councils, which implied that the Standing Conference could determine CCJ's policy. There was, for example, a question whether *Common Ground* should be continued. Simpson thought that this was a matter for the Executive, who should decide whether they wished to ask the Standing Conference's opinion.

Meeting of the Standing Conference and the National Executive

In October 1972, at the Tenth Meeting of the Standing Conference, at which Rev. Robert Richards, of Hendon and Golders Green, was in the chair, it was reported that the Executive had agreed to a meeting of representatives of the Standing Conference and the National Executive. The intention was that the meeting should be for a period of 24 hours, from Sunday afternoon to Monday lunchtime. The Standing Conference chose its representatives. It also expressed the hope that the meeting might take place before the end of 1973, as the matters were urgent. It will be recalled that this was a time of severe financial difficulties in the life of the Council. It was suggested that a background document be prepared.

Partly because of staff changes, the process of consultation became protracted. A preliminary consultation was held on 15 October 1974; it prepared a discussion paper, which was so 'Strictly Confidential' that each copy was numbered. A major issue was Israel. Some people had been critical of the Council for its 'alleged' silence during the Yom Kippur War. The taboo on theological dialogue was also questioned. The lack of an Education Officer was another concern. Local councils also wanted to know if they could make statements to the press on their own authority.

Before proceeding to the consultation, which was to be held at Exbury, the Executive agreed with the Standing Conference that a further preliminary meeting should be arranged. It was decided to hold this in April 1975, but in the end it was cancelled because 'despite our best efforts to pick a suitable date, the number of apologies for absence ultimately made the meeting impracticable'.[6] Shortly afterwards, the Executive decided to cancel the Exbury Consultation itself. Instead, it was agreed that the meeting of the Standing Conference scheduled for 15 October should take the form of a full-scale consultation between the entire Standing Conference and the entire Executive Committee. Prior to that meeting, Dr Levy, Mr Palin, Rev. Robert Richards, Ven. Carl Witton-Davies and Peter Jennings met to identify the key issues. The 'most fraught issue', in Dr Levy's words, 'is the constitution of CCJ which gives only Members of Council (140) the right to elect the Executive. Associate members, numbering 3,000 approx, over half of whom are attached to local councils, are not even mentioned in the constitution.'[7]

The consultation on 15 October 1975 tackled many of the contentious issues. It was recognised that the dividing line between political and social and moral comment was a very thin one. It was agreed that local councils could issue statements to the press, provided it was made clear that these were only in the name of a particular local council. On the constitutional issue, it was agreed to adjust and enlarge the membership of the Council, rather than make major changes to the constitution. The worrying financial position provoked a long discussion and it was eventually agreed to double the subscription from £1 to £2. Dr Levy voiced his concern about the lack of policy direction and said it was essential to have 'working parties' of qualified people to advise on key issues.

Constitutional Changes

In 1977, some constitutional changes were made which were one more step towards democracy. They were designed to stop the Executive being a self-perpetuating body. It was agreed to increase the number of elected members of the Executive to 16. It was also decided that two Jews and two Christians should retire annually. Retiring members could not immediately stand for re-election. A suggestion that a similar limitation should apply to officers was rejected.

At last, in 1982, the old oligarchic structure was swept away. Membership of the Council was opened to 'all persons who subscribe to the purposes of the Council'. The officers, who are the joint honorary secretaries and treasurers, as well as the joint presidents and the vice-presidents, and the members of the Executive were now to be elected by the enlarged membership. The chairman and vice-chairmen continue to be chosen by the Executive Committee itself.

Efforts to involve Local Councils

Even though by the 1980s the structure of CCJ had become democratic, members of local councils still did not feel fully involved in the Council's activities. Further efforts have, therefore, been made to alleviate this feeling. In part this has been achieved by regular visits to councils, although central office staff have to wait to be invited – and some councils which complain that they never see

11. Bishop Gerald Mahon, Rev. Dr Edward Carpenter and Rev. Dr R. Craig

12. A Seder demonstration at Southport CCJ

13. Paul Mendel and Sister Margaret Shepherd

anyone from the central office also never issue invitations! In part, a deliberate effort has been made to obtain news of their activities from local councils and to include this in the CCJ Newsletter and now in *Common Ground*.

Fairly successful attempts have been made to attract larger attendances at meetings of the Standing Conference of Local Councils. A representative of B'nai B'rith regularly attends. Besides the necessary business, a major item of interest has been included in the agenda. One of the first experiments in this new direction was to offer those attending the meeting the opportunity to take part in a tour of Jewish London.

The annual general meeting of the Standing Conference is now held each year in a different venue, outside London. London members initially resisted my suggestion, but now they look forward to an 'annual outing'. The business meeting has been combined with a day conference. In addition the local council has provided overnight hospitality and arranged a visit to places of interest in its area. By this means, the local council has been strengthened and encouraged and those who attend regularly get a picture of CCJ's work in different parts of the country. Very successful local council conferences have been held in various cities, including Nottingham, Liverpool and Sheffield.

In October 1990, the conference was held in Glasgow, which that year was the European City of Culture. Participants arrived in time for an evening meal with their hosts. The conference then began with an address by the Moderator of the General Assembly of the Church of Scotland, the Very Rev. Dr W. McDonald. This was given at Garnethill Synagogue, which is the oldest synagogue in Scotland. It was built in 1879 and is now the home of the Scottish Jewish Archives Centre.

On the following day there was a visit to Ross Priory, Gartocharn, on the shore of beautiful Loch Lomond. The main business session was then held at the Jewish Welfare Board Council Chambers. The next day, for those who could stay on, there was a visit to Kelvingrove Art Galleries to see the 'Treasures of the Holy Land Exhibition' from the Israel Museum.

Further Constitutional Changes

With the change to the constitution in 1982, which made all 'associate members' members of the Council, CCJ had become a democratic body. Even so, many who lived outside London still found it hard to play an active part nationally in the Council's affairs. The proportion of members of the Executive who live outside London has, however, grown. One difficulty was whether the Council could afford to pay the travelling expenses of those attending meetings. A postal ballot has been introduced for elections to the Executive – although in its first year this was unnecessary, as the nominations were exactly equal to the vacancies! Recently the decision has been made to increase the number of Executive Committee meetings from four to six each year. At two of these discussion will concentrate on a major item of policy, rather than on detailed business. Invited members will only be asked to attend 'policy' meetings. At least one of the six meetings is to be held outside London.

It was finance which brought the continuing difficulties in the relationship of local councils to the national Executive to a head. In 1984 subscriptions were increased to £5 per annum. It was agreed that 60 per cent would be retained by the central office and 40 per cent returned to the local council, where a member belonged to such a council. In September 1987, the subscription was doubled to £10. This caused considerable ill-feeling. It was felt that local councils had not been adequately consulted. Some long established councils complained that a number of their older members had resigned, although it was made clear that the figure was the normal subscription and that concessionary membership was available. Newer branches seemed to have fewer problems.[8]

Difficulties had been exacerbated by the introduction of a computer at central office. This made it easy for subscriptions to be collected nationally, which was already the agreed policy, but some councils felt their autonomy was being eroded.[9] The difficulty was that a local treasurer might know an individual member's circumstances, whereas a computer demands a standardised system.

Some of the unease of local councils was voiced at a meeting of the Standing Conference, held in the early summer of 1988. Canon Richardson, realising the importance of good relations with local branches, immediately took action. As a result, the Executive agreed to set up a small working party to look at the issues.[10] By the following summer, the report and suggestions of the working party had been agreed at a meeting of the Standing Conference. The recommendations were fully discussed at a meeting of the Executive, held on 20 September 1989. Presenting the report, Rev. Dr Tom Broadbent, who is chairman of the Manchester council, said that local councils felt that their advice about subscriptions had been ignored. Clarification of the term 'council' was needed and local councils wanted more flexibility and more involvement in the elections to the Executive.

After a long discussion, the Executive, responding positively to the suggestions made, set up a sub-committee to examine them and to suggest necessary alterations to the constitution.[11]

These constitutional amendments were presented to the 1990 annual general meeting and accepted. Penny Faust and Sidney Shipton, in an article in *Common Ground*, summed up the changes.

> First, that the Association be called an Association of Local Branches, not of Local Councils and that it be recognised specifically in the Constitution. Secondly, that Annual Subscriptions be determined from time to time by the AGM of members not the Executive. Thirdly, that unnecessary verbiage as to transitional provisions be abbreviated. Fourthly, that absentees without good reason from four consecutive Executive Committee meetings 'shall forfeit their membership'. Fifthly, obvious omissions in the list of Honorary Officers in the appropriate clause have been rectified. Sixthly, the technical financial powers clauses passed at the previous AGM (allowing CCJ to own property) have been incorporated appropriately into the constitution.

Reduced subscription rates for pensioners and the unwaged were now made clear and postal votes for elections to the executive were introduced.[12]

It is to be hoped that all the work put into these revisions will resolve a problem that has been with CCJ from the beginning – a problem encountered also by other similar bodies which work both at international, national and local levels. A variety of subscription rates has now been set. Even so, the year's subscription is less than many people will spend on one meal out. Whilst CCJ is clearly not a missionary society, it is sad that many members think of their subscription in terms of what they get for it, rather than as a donation to further the cause of Jewish–Christian understanding. A large proportion of subscriptions are returned to local councils and the other half does not fully meet the cost of the mailings which members receive and copies of Common Ground – although the hope is that this will be financed by advertisements. CCJ exists because of the generosity of some individual benefactors and donations from some trusts, particularly the Group Relations Educational Trust, not, in most cases, because of the giving of individual members.

SOME LOCAL COUNCILS

There is not room to give a history of all the local councils. Their work, however, has been vital in transforming Jewish–Christian relations in Britain. Through them new developments have reached members of churches and synagogues and local schools. The many friendships made typify the best achievements of CCJ. Some local branches date back to the Second World War, whilst others are quite new. Perhaps some councils will arrange for their history to be written as a contribution to CCJ's Fiftieth Anniversary.

1944

In 1944, Rev. Dr E.L. Allen was asked to speak to the national Council about the work of local councils. His talk, in effect, was a description of what was happening in Newcastle-upon-Tyne. There were three dimensions in which, he said, the Council had tried to work: religious, educational and spiritual. The Christian ministers had wanted an opportunity to learn about Judaism as a living faith. They had attended a service at the synagogue and were studying the Jewish Prayer Book with the help of a Jewish minister. With the help of the University, the Council had arranged some public lectures. Dr Cecil Roth had given a brilliant talk on the History of the Jews. They were also arranging programmes with the Workers' Educational Association (WEA). In one mining village in Northumberland, a group had spent 12 weeks studying the Jewish problem. The Council was also trying to bring young Jews and Christians together in social activities. The Council, on the advice of its Jewish members, had not concentrated on openly combating antisemitism. Instead, 'the emphasis had been on building up those habits of mind which . . . will make anti-Jewish feeling impossible'.[13]

1947

A summary of local activity, prepared in 1947, shows interesting differences in the response to antisemitism. Brighton reported that antisemitism had been evident there for 15 years and was growing, because of the situation in Palestine. The British League of Ex-Servicemen and Women, a right wing group, was planning a series of open-air meetings and the local CCJ had voiced their concern about this to the police. Leeds recorded prejudice, especially amongst the middle classes. Because of a lack of public sympathy, the Council's work was restricted to providing speakers when asked to do so. It did not arrange any public meetings itself. In Manchester too, prejudice was noted amongst members of both the middle and working classes and it was reported that a monthly magazine praising Hitler was widely distributed. In Teesside, Sunderland and South Shields little anti-semitism was reported. The same was true of Newcastle-upon-Tyne, although no Jew could become a member of a golf club in the area. In Birmingham, where relations were good, the Council had concentrated on bringing a really representative group of people together in case action should prove necessary. No attempt had been made to recruit a large membership. By contrast, Cardiff had a full-time organizing secretary and a membership of 480. In 1946 and 1947, 42 meetings had been addressed in the area and the Executive itself had met every month.[14]

1962

Fifteen years later, at the first conference of Local Council Representatives, another summary picture of their work is provided. In Manchester, Brotherhood Week was already a major event. The Manchester Council had been formed in the 1940s, under the leadership of the Bishops of Manchester and of Salford, the chairman of the Free Church Federal Council and with one of the Manchester rabbis as another joint president. Brotherhood Week, or Friendship Week as it is now called, has usually included a concert, a big public meeting and services at churches or synagogues, to which visitors are welcomed. Brochures and reports on the Manchester Brotherhood Week were available at the 1962 meeting. At the time there was some discussion whether it should be taken up nationally. Eventually the national Executive decided against this, but some other councils, especially in North London, started to arrange similar weeks. Rev. Paul Guinness also mentioned the importance that the Manchester council attached to school conferences. These, like Brotherhood Week, have continued. Liverpool had only a small Jewish community, but there was great friendship between Jews and Christians. There has long been a lively council there.

In London, Hampstead was one of the first local councils to be established. This was in 1947, on the initiative of Anthony (later Lord) Greenwood, Bea (later Baroness) Serota and Rev. Dr I. Levy. The council has enjoyed the cooperation of major organisations in the borough. Every successive Mayor has served as honorary president. In its early years the council concentrated on addresses by trio teams, consisting of a Catholic, a Protestant and a Jewish speaker. A special feature of the programme was recitals of liturgical music. Willesden council had been formed in 1951, but felt overshadowed by Hampstead and found it difficult to persuade clergy to attend meetings regularly. Edgware was, at the time of the meeting, quite a new council, having been formed in 1960. It had already had two successful public meetings. Finchley council, which we shall describe more fully below, had just come into being, as had the Hendon and Golders Green council, which owes so much to the enthusiasm of Mrs Rose Owen, although efforts at Christian–Jewish cooperation in the area dated back to the early 1930s. Wimbledon and District council was started in the early 1950s by Sir Cyril Black and some friends. For a time it was a particularly active branch with support from several churches and synagogues. Now, the membership is rather elderly.

In the north-east of England, Hull council was established in 1949. Its tenth anniversary was marked by a banquet, held under the chairmanship of the Lord Mayor, at which Dr Michael Ramsey, then Archbishop of York, and Dr S. Gaon, the Haham, had spoken. Leeds council had been formed one year before Hull. Leeds gave a lot of attention to work with children and arranged visits to synagogues. Usually an annual lecture was given by a distinguished speaker.

In Wales, Cardiff continued active and a Swansea council was formed in 1961. The Bournemouth council was formed in 1963.[15]

Continued Growth

The number of local councils has steadily increased, so that now there are nearly 50. They are listed in Appendix Five. The activities are very varied, including social events, such as garden parties. Often members attend festival celebrations or visit places of worship. Talks are given on a very wide range of topics. Sometimes they are on historical matters, sometimes on theological issues and sometimes on contemporary matters of debate.

* * *

Rather than attempt a general description, it may be better to give a detailed picture of the efforts to establish one particular council, namely Nottingham, and then to mention, almost at random, a few other councils.

Nottingham

Efforts to form a council in Nottingham were protracted. Much of the correspondence has been preserved and the letters illustrate the difficulties which enthusiasts for the CCJ have often encountered also in other places.

In 1943, Rachel Hetherington invited Simpson to speak at a lunch-hour meeting of the Union of Students at the University. The detailed correspondence about Simpson's travel arrangements and the notes for his talk survive. Beginning with comments on the dire situation in Germany, Simpson traced the origins of antisemitism. He made clear that its roots lay deep in Christian teaching, which had often forgotten that Jesus was a Jew and which had failed to appreciate Pharisaic and Rabbinic teaching.

Following the meeting, which was in May, Simpson wrote to Rev. J. Dobson, the Secretary of Nottinghamshire Christian Council, enquiring about the possibility of forming a CCJ.

Eventually, in the autumn, Simpson received a reply. The Council had discussed his letter and whilst it was not in favour of setting up a Council of Christians and Jews, it agreed to informal liaison with the Jewish community, represented by the local rabbi, Dr Goldman. Mr Dobson was at pains to point out the 'large

111

number of matters' that the Council already had in hand. Simpson, in acknowledging the letter, sent some copies of two CCJ pamphlets. In May 1944, almost exactly a year after the meeting with the Union of Students, Simpson sent Mr Goldman copies of the second issue of CCJ's *Occasional Review* for distribution to those who might be interested. Mr Dobson, with refreshing honesty, admitted that he had not yet contacted Dr Goldman, but explained that he was unwell for some of the winter (it was now May!) and that he was 'loaded with work'. Meanwhile, Simpson had received information about some links between the Nottingham Jewish Youth Club and the YMCA. Simpson also wrote to Dr Goldman to prepare him for an approach from Mr Dobson. The position, however, remained that Christian–Jewish relations in Nottingham were considered to be quite good, and that informal liaison rather than a CCJ was all that was required. It is a little sad that CCJs were only thought necessary when relations were bad!

In 1950, when Simpson again visited Nottingham, the position was unchanged. He was invited to meet the Vice-Chancellor and Professor John Marsh of the Department of Theology. The latter seems to have been rather offended by the implication that Christian theology could possibly be anti-Jewish! He appears to have regarded the Ten Points of Seelisberg, which Simpson showed him, as a personal attack. 'Be assured', Professor Marsh wrote, 'we shall try to be scrupulously honest with our studies of the events that lie at the heart of the Christian story.' Professor Marsh said that the University would guard against any signs of antisemitism and seemed to imply that the establishment of a CCJ would draw attention to this evil. In response, Simpson spoke of the 'largely unconscious prejudice on the part of many Christians'.

In 1962, Simpson tried again. He was invited by Mr Millett to speak to the Nottingham B'nai B'rith on 2 October. The Jewish leaders mentioned their hope that more contact could be established with local Christians. Simpson therefore wrote to various Christian leaders in Nottingham. Canon Douglas Feaver, of St Mary's, Nottingham, said he was 'not enthusiastic for starting another council in Nottingham', but agreed to invite some clergy to tea to meet Simpson. The evening meeting of the B'nai B'rith was very successful. Afterwards, Simpson met with some of the officers of the synagogue. He explained that at the afternoon meeting, the clergy had been against trying to set up a council.

They felt that the small Jewish community was 'well and happily integrated into the life of the city' and that to establish a formal organisation 'might well be misinterpreted as implying the existence of a problem where in fact no problem was immediately apparent'. The Jewish community were, however, interested in a formal organisation for two main reasons. The first was that it would be of value for members of each community to have a better understanding of the other's background and point of view and, second, because of the possibility of racist agitation in a city with a considerable population of 'coloured immigrants'.

In a letter to Mr Strauss, of B'nai B'rith, early in 1963, Simpson said that he had heard from Rabbi Posen, who felt on the whole it was not necessary to have a special organisation concerned with Christian–Jewish relations. Canon Feaver had also said that he entirely agreed with Rabbi Posen and felt there was no point in pursuing the matter further. Mr Strauss, however, did not let the idea rest. 'We may be slow in moving here in the Midlands, but we certainly do not give up easily.' He managed to interest local Rotary Clubs in the matter, hoping that more success would be achieved through 'secular organisations'. He also gained support for his initiative from the Society of Friends.

Thanks to the help of Mr P. G. Phillips and other Friends, a meeting was held at the Friends' Meeting House on 26 April 1965, at which the speaker was the Rev. J. E. Sexton, CCJ's organising secretary. The only Anglican clergyman to attend was Professor A. R. C. Leaney of Nottingham University, whose own studies on the New Testament and the Dead Sea Scrolls have made a significant contribution to Christian–Jewish understanding. There is a little confusion as to whether this was the 'inaugural meeting'. The April meeting decided to form a council and chose a committee. Thereafter an approach was made to religious leaders in the area, who were sympathetic. A public meeting was held on 26 October 1965, at which the Bishop of Southwell, Rt Rev. Gordon Savage, agreed to speak, as did a representative of the Roman Catholic Bishop of Nottingham, Free Church leaders and also Rabbi Posen. The Lord Mayor presided. Bishop Savage spoke of his detestation of all forms of prejudice. He said it was a sign of the good relations that already existed that a council was being formed. The council was not being set up because there were problems.

At last, rather more than 20 years after Simpson had first spoken in Nottingham, a Nottingham CCJ was in existence. There were still problems ahead. The cards collected at the public meeting, with the names and addresses of those who were interested, were lost. A meeting in 1967 only had an audience of seven and when, a little while afterwards, only three people turned up to a committee meeting, the newly formed council nearly collapsed. A few stalwarts persisted and the 1968 AGM, at which the speaker was Archdeacon Witton-Davies, was well attended. It was in 1968, also, that Mrs Elisabeth Hitchman, whose enthusiasm for the council has been unflagging, became an office holder.

The council has over the years had an interesting and varied programme. In 1968, Rabbi Dr Goldman returned to address the AGM. The following year, the speaker was the Bishop of Southwell. Other speakers have included W.W. Simpson, Peter Jennings, Dr Albert Friedlander and Mr Hyam Maccoby.[16]

Finchley

Finchley has always been an active council. The Finchley branch was founded in 1961 by Frank Gibson, during his first period of office as Mayor of Finchley, although the idea of a Finchley council originates from the late Marcus King. At a meeting held in the Mayor's Parlour a film was shown by the local Zionist Society about Buchenwald concentration camp. After the showing, the whole audience was silent in complete horror. Frank mounted the stage and in a moving address announced that he proposed to establish a Finchley branch of CCJ. A committee was formed and Rev. R. Douglas became the first chairman. In due course, Frank Gibson, who was later awarded the OBE for his many services to the borough, became for several years chairman and then a vice-president.

Of the original committee, only Monsignor More O'Ferrall and Mrs Queenie Weber survive. Msgr More O'Ferrall has always been a source of encouragement and good advice. Queenie Weber, who has served on the national Executive, has been chairman and is now a vice-president.

The branch has at present some 170 members. Each summer, a Friendship Week is held. During this Jewish members attend a

114

church service and Christian members come to a synagogue. A public meeting is arranged most months.[17]

Redbridge

Redbridge council also dates from the 1960s. The inaugural meeting was held at Ilford Town Hall on 11 May 1965, and the first AGM was held the following year at Ilford Synagogue. There are still half a dozen members who were at these meetings.

Each year, the council has a visit to a Succoth, arranges a demonstration Seder and has a social occasion to mark Hannukah and Christmas. An Annual Choir Festival has been held every year since 1967. A 'Quiz' meeting is a regular part of the programme. The meetings are held in different parts of this widely scattered borough. Recently, the council has helped the Religious Education Adviser mount a Sixth-Form day conference. Regular study/discussion groups are held in members' houses. An interesting newsletter, edited by Neil Macdonald, who is a tireless worker for CCJ, is produced regularly.

Avon

Avon is one of the newer councils, although there was some CCJ activity in the area in the 1950s. In the early 1970s, Albert Polack and I helped to form a branch of the World Congress of Faiths in the area and Tony Reese, of the Bristol and West Progressive Synagogue, has over the years maintained interfaith activity in the area. In the early 1980s, the time seemed right to form a local CCJ as well. The Bishop of Bristol, Dr Barry Rogerson, had been invited to speak at the Orthodox Synagogue. He took the opportunity to suggest that a local CCJ would be useful. The idea was taken up and a public meeting was arranged for 23 November 1987. This was held at the Bristol synagogue, with Rabbi Dr Norman Solomon as the speaker. The meeting was widely advertised and, in the event, the room was crowded. It was agreed to form a local council and a steering committee was chosen.

The council has benefited from the enthusiastic support of the Bristol and West Progressive Synagogue. The Synagogue's rabbi, Rabbi Ronald Francis Berry, is now co-chairman. Initially, the council was helped by Clifton College, where there is a Jewish house. Rabbi Michael Morris, of the Orthodox synagogue, has also been supportive and the Council has also benefited from links with the Ammerdown Conference Centre in the area.

Meetings are held in both Bristol and Bath. Emphasis has been placed on members getting to know each other well. There have been social occasions and visits have been made to different religious centres, including Wells Cathedral. Joint times of bible study have proved especially fruitful.

CONCLUSION

St Paul ends many of his letters with a long list of names of people to whom he sends greetings. I am tempted to do the same, as I recall the friendship and hospitality of members of so many local councils – some of which like the enthusiastic Cambridge University Council or the well-established Southport Council have not even been mentioned by name. Inevitably any history tends to describe external events, but it is in the friendships made, the prejudices dispelled and the insights gained that the true achievements of CCJ are reflected. Above all, these have been the accomplishments of local branches.

9

International Involvement

From the very beginning, CCJ has been involved in the world-wide struggle to build a new relationship between Jews and Christians. This is partly because the issues are international – events in Israel, or the proposal to build a Carmelite convent at Auschwitz, which many Jews found offensive, had international repercussions. It is also because of Britain's role in world affairs. When the Council was formed, London was still the heart of the Empire. Another reason for this international concern is that members of the Churches in Britain also thereby belong to world-wide confessional bodies, which may also themselves belong to the World Council of Churches. The world-wide Jewish community also has a great sense of solidarity. Members of CCJ have taken a leading role in establishing contacts with those working in this field in other countries. Quite recently, for example, when plans were being made to form a Victoria Council of Christians and Jews in Australia, advice was sought from CCJ.

W.W. Simpson and Ruth Weyl have already written an admirable *Brief History of the International Council of Christians and Jews*. I have summarised much of this material in my history of the interfaith movement, *Pilgrimage of Hope*.[2] It is unnecessary, therefore, here to repeat in full the history of the formation and growth of ICCJ. Yet, without some account of these developments, an important aspect of CCJ's activities will be missing. The international involvements of members of CCJ have also been shown through the participation of members of CCJ in other international meetings for dialogue.

117

War-time

One Sunday evening during the blitz in 1942, a small group of Jews and Christians from Britain and America dined together at the Savoy Hotel in London. The American guests were Fr Edward Cardinal, a Catholic priest, Rabbi Morris Lazaron and Rev Everett Clinchy, who was president of the National Conference of Christians and Jews (NCCJ). They had come to study the effect of the blitz on the morale of the British people. Naturally enough, conversation turned to the work of NCCJ and of CCJ, which had just been established.[1]

In March 1943, an extraordinary meeting of the Council was held to listen to Rabbi Dr Israel Goldstein, who was president of the Synagogue Council of the USA and on the board of NCCJ.[3] He said he was glad to find considerable interest in Britain in the Three-Faith Declaration, drawn up in America, which set out seven points as a basis for international peace. Soon after this meeting, CCJ publicly endorsed the Declaration.[4] Dr Goldstein also talked about how NCCJ was trying to combat antisemitism in the USA. He mentioned their 'Round Table' meetings, their 'Brotherhood Week' and their surveys of textbooks. Towards the end of the meeting, 'the feeling was expressed by all present that one of the first things to be done after the war would be to hold an International Conference representative of the various bodies at work in the field of Jewish–Christian relations in order to secure closer co-operation and better understanding of the problem'.[5]

The Oxford Conference 1946

A considerable amount of the time and energy of the Executive and staff during the next months was given to preparing for this international conference. Oxford was the chosen venue and the conference met there at Lady Margaret Hall in August 1946.

Representatives of other existing organisations for understanding between Jews and Christians were invited. For example, Alan Paton, who two years later was to write his famous book, *Cry the Beloved Country*, represented the South African Society of Jews and Christians, which had been formed in the 1930s, but which soon after the Oxford conference was to wither in a climate hostile to its purposes. Individuals from other European countries, where there was no organisation, were also invited. In all, there were well over 100 participants from 15 countries. Special permission was obtained to include two Christian pastors from Germany, Dean Gruber from Berlin and Hermann Maas from Heidelberg. A Jewish participant, several years later, described their presence as 'profoundly impressive – one might say traumatic'.[6]

On the eve of the conference, a crowded public meeting was held in London. Speakers included the Archbishop of Canterbury, the theologian, Professor Reinhold Niebuhr, the politician, R. A. Butler and Rabbi Dr Leo Baeck. The latter's appeal for tolerance and understanding, so soon after his release from the Theresienstadt concentration camp, made an unforgettable impression.

The theme of the Conference was 'Freedom, Justice and Responsibility'. Considerable preparatory work was done and much of the time was spent in six commissions. A youth commission was also formed. The commissions' reports were published. The second commission agreed a declaration on 'Fundamental Postulates of Judaism and Christianity in Relation to Social Order', which Dr W. R. Matthews, the Dean of St Paul's Cathedral, said was of 'considerable interest for all who are concerned about the future of civilised man'. A resolution was sent to the Paris Peace Conference.

Two other decisions were made at Oxford. It was agreed to hold an emergency conference as soon as possible on the problem of antisemitism in Europe. It was also agreed that a 'Continuation Committee be set up to make plans for the establishment of an International Council of Christians and Jews', but this was not to be fulfilled for nearly 30 years.[7]

Seelisberg

The emergency conference was held at Seelisberg, in Switzerland, in 1947. It is chiefly remembered for 'The Ten Points of Seelisberg'. They are an address to the Churches and have served as the basis for many Catholic and Protestant statements on a new Christian approach to Judaism.[8] The Seelisberg conference also urged that the Oxford suggestion of an International Council of Christians and Jews 'should be implemented without delay'.

The next year, a constitution for an international council was adopted. But when it came to the ratification of this by national councils, problems arose. The British, French, German and Swiss organisations all agreed. NCCJ, however, decided not to ratify the constitution. Everett Clinchy, despite his initial enthusiasm, had come to feel that the use of 'Christian' in their titles by some European political parties, would mean that those of other political persuasion would not support the new body, which included Christian in its title. He felt a more broadly based organisation was necessary to combat antisemitism and racism and now put his energies into World Brotherhood. This put an end, for nearly 20 years, to any plans for an international council.

Maintaining International Contacts

Simpson did what he could to maintain international contacts. There was regular correspondence with 'World Brotherhood'. Although no formal links were established, Simpson attended some of the meetings arranged by World Brotherhood. He also kept in touch with other national councils in Europe. These included the French Amitié Judéo-Chrétienne, the German Coordinating Council (DKR), the Austrian Aktion gegen den Antisemitismus, the Amicizia Ebraico-Cristiana in Florence, a Swiss group and CCJ. Thanks largely to the work of Simpson, a series of private and informal meetings took place, out of which grew an Informal Liaison Committee of Secretaries of Organisations of Christians and Jews. In December 1960, at a meeting in London, it was agreed to review the role of the Liaison Committee and its secretariat. By this time an Israel Committee for Interfaith Understanding had been formed. Israel included a wide religious mixture, with Jews from many countries and of many traditions, Christians of almost all denominations, Muslims and members of smaller religions such as the Druze and Baha'is. Christian–Jewish organisations had also been established in Argentina and Uruguay.

The International Consultative Council

Eventually in 1962 the time was ripe to form an International Consultative Committee of organisations concerned with Christian–Jewish cooperation. That such a move had not been possible earlier was largely because of the dominant theological climate amongst Protestants which was unsympathetic to interfaith understanding, and because of Catholic suspicions that Christian–Jewish organisations were 'indifferentist'.

The International Consultative Committee of Organisations working for Christian–Jewish Cooperation was formally established at a meeting at Frankfurt in January 1962. Its main objective was to provide for 'consultation between member organisations on matters of common concern in the field of Christian–Jewish relations'.[9] It could recommend action, but had no authority over member groups. At last, in 1974, NCCJ joined and, at its suggestion, the name of the organisation was changed to the International Council of Christians and Jews. Simpson, who had been general secretary of the Consultative Committee, became the unpaid secretary of the new Council. As he had by this time retired as general secretary of CCJ, he was able to bring his great energy and experience to this task, ably supported by Ruth Weyl, his part-time secretarial assistant.

Cambridge 1966

In 1966, the International Consultative Committee held a major international conference in Cambridge. This also marked the 20th anniversary of the first international conference which had been held at Oxford in 1946. Although the conference was only half the size of the Oxford meeting, several eminent scholars and leaders attended. These included Fr Edward Flannery, Dr Samuel Sandmel, Alice and Roy Eckardt and Rabbi Marc Tannenbaum from the USA and Dr James Parkes, Ven. C. Witton-Davies and Rabbi Dr I. Levy, from Britain.

The conference issued a critique of the Vatican II Declaration *Nostra Aetate* and of the WCC New Delhi statement on Christian relations with the Jews. It also produced a definition of dialogue, which is still of value.

> The dialogue is essentially a dialogue between persons, an attitude to life and not a mere technique. It is a relationship which has been found in experience to be capable of deepening the spiritual life of all participants alike, for each is given in dialogue full opportunity to express his own position in all freedom. It has proved an enrichment of their faith in God to committed Jews and Christians, and has dispelled many misunderstandings of each about the faith and practice of the other. We believe that it is not only consistent with our several loyalties to Church and Synagogue, but that it also increases

121

interreligious harmony as we face together the problems and needs of our changing world.[10]

The International Council of Christians and Jews

In 1975 the International Council of Christians and Jews (ICCJ), as it was now officially known, met in Hamburg. In 1976 ICCJ met in Jerusalem and focused on the significance of Israel in Jewish–Christian dialogue. In 1977 it was held in Southampton, England, to celebrate Parkes' 80th birthday and to commemorate the centenary of the birth of Jules Isaac – two scholars who had made an ineradicable contribution to building a new relationship between Jews and Christians. The conference was also the occasion of the official opening at the University of Southampton of the Parkes Library, which holds the remarkable collection of books and pamphlets on Christian–Jewish relations that James Parkes had gathered together.

A conference or 'colloquium', as it was usually called, now became an annual event. CCJ has always been well represented at these gatherings and is to host the 1991 Colloquium, which is once more to be held at Southampton in July. The subject will be 'When Religion is Used as a Weapon . . . The Use and Misuse of Religion in Defence of National and Fundamental Values'. Speakers will include Rt Rev. Richard Harries, Bishop of Oxford, Rabbi David Rosen of the Sapir Jewish Heritage Centre in Jerusalem and Dr Mohammed Shaalan, Professor of Psychiatry at Al-Azhar University, Cairo. The Colloquium will include a visit to Winchester and a concert by the Southampton Chamber Orchestra.

In 1979, Sir Sigmund Sternberg, who was joint treasurer of CCJ in Britain, was elected chairman of the Executive of ICCJ. He has brought great energy and enthusiasm as well as wide contacts to ICCJ and helped to give the work a higher profile. In 1985 this was recognised when the Pope made him a Knight of the Order of St Gregory – only the second Jew to receive so high an honour. The Orthodox Churches have also honoured him by making him a member of the Order of St John. Sir Sigmund played a major role in helping to defuse the controversy about the convent at Auschwitz. Another leading member of CCJ to make a major contribution to ICCJ is Lord Coggan, who is honorary president. Dr Elisabeth Maxwell is a vice-president and Ruth Weyl, too, has continued her active interest as minute secretary and consultant editor of *ICCJ News*.

In the same year as Sir Sigmund became chairman, it was agreed to appoint Dr Jacobus (Coss) Schoneveld, a Pastor of the Netherlands Reformed Church who had studied for several years in Israel, as general secretary. This had by now become a full-time paid post. The offices had by then moved to Martin Buber House in Heppenheim, Germany.

International Youth Conferences

The initiative for the first international youth conference was taken by CCJ. In 1977, an international youth conference was arranged in Wales. Subsequent youth gatherings arranged by ICCJ in Israel, Switzerland and elsewhere have been well supported by CCJ. In 1991, an ICCJ Young Leadership Conference will again be held in Britain, prior to the ICCJ Colloquium. There will also be an ICCJ Women's Seminar.[11]

WORKING WITH THE CHURCHES

Besides active involvement in ICCJ and its predecessors, CCJ has kept abreast of developments in Christian–Jewish relations at the World Council of Churches, at the Vatican and in other Churches. Indeed some members have played a part in influencing these developments.

The World Council of Churches

At its first assembly in Amsterdam in 1948, the World Council of Churches (WCC) denounced antisemitism. WCC has had a continuing concern to improve Christian–Jewish relations, even if its political comments on the Middle East situation have often annoyed Jews and Christian friends of Israel. CCJ has exercised what influence it can on WCC deliberations. Simpson attended the 1947 Amsterdam Assembly as an observer. On his return, the Executive had so much other business that it did not have time to listen to his report! Following the 1954 Evanston Assembly, a conference was held at Bossey, Switzerland, which Simpson attended. From this conference came into being the Churches Consultation on the Jewish People, which has met periodically and produced various influential statements on the subject. Simpson was a member of this, as have been other members of CCJ, such as Peter Schneider, Eric Allen and myself.[12] I attended the Vancouver Assembly of the WCC as an observer for the World Congress of Faiths, and Sir Sigmund Sternberg attended the 1991 Canberra Assembly.

The Vatican

The importance of the Roman Catholic Church in Christian–Jewish relations cannot be underestimated. The difficulties of the 1950s have already been described. The position was transformed by the Second Vatican Council's Declaration *Nostra Aetate*. This, in the words of Gerhard Riegner, who for many years was secretary general of the World Jewish Congress, 'definitely closes the era of friction and enmity'.[13] Subsequent Vatican documents have amplified this teaching. CCJ, often in partnership with the Sisters of Sion, has been influential in Britain in helping to make these developments widely known. Some people from Britain have also taken part in official conversations of the International Catholic–Jewish Liaison Committee. Participants have included Bishop Burke of Salford, who was for some years chairman of the Secretariat for Catholic–Jewish Relations of the Bishops' Conference of England and Wales, Rabbi Louis Jacobs, Rev. Graham Jenkins and Rabbi Dr Norman Solomon.

CCJ too has had its own direct relations with the Vatican. A group from CCJ visited Rome in 1980 and was received at a public audience. In 1990, a small delegation was received in private audience. CCJ expressed its concern about the resurgence of anti-semitism, especially in Eastern Europe. It hoped that His Holiness would continue to speak out against racism, extremism and fundamentalism. In his reply, the Pope assured CCJ of his support 'in continuing actively to foster friendly dialogue, brotherly understanding, and the exchange of spiritual values at the national level'. He spoke too of the urgent need for peace and of his sorrow for the peoples of the Holy Land.[14]

The Anglican Communion

Other members of CCJ have been active in their own particular Churches. CCJ was well represented at the two official Anglican–

Jewish consultations. The first was held at Amport House, Andover from 26 to 28 November 1980. The theme was 'Law and Religion in Contemporary Society'. The consultation was chaired by the Archbishop of York, Stuart Blanch and by the Chief Rabbi, Dr Jakobovits.[15] The second consultation was held at Shallowford House near Stafford from 27 to 29 April 1987. The emphasis was on the responsibilities of the two communities with regard to major social concerns, including AIDS and the inner cities.[16]

At the Lambeth Conference in 1988, the Bishops of the Anglican Communion agreed a document called *Jews, Christians and Muslims: The Way of Dialogue*. Much of the preparatory work was done in Britain by a group led by the Rt Rev. Richard Harries, which included Rabbi Dr Norman Solomon, Rev. Dr John Bowden, Sister Margaret Shepherd and myself. Immediately prior to the conference's debate on this paper, CCJ hosted a dinner for some of the bishops to explain the issues involved. This, I soon discovered, was more necessary than I had realised. I sat next to a bishop from the islands of the South Pacific Ocean, who asked me more than once whether the rabbi opposite was a Christian! A long-standing member of the CCJ Executive said that the dinner together with the information circulated beforehand was arguably the most useful thing CCJ had ever done.

In the debate some of the bishops, especially from Africa, seemed to think dialogue and evangelisation belonged together, so the document was adopted unanimously. Even so, it is a statement of major significance and CCJ has worked hard to inform members of the Church of England of this pronouncement of their bishops.[16] CCJ has also urged leaders of the Churches, especially the Anglican Consultative Council, to follow up the recommendations.[17]

The Lambeth Conference's discussion of the Israel/Palestine issue was in the end more balanced than at one time seemed likely. A preparatory document issued by the Anglican Consultative Council totally identified with the Palestinian case. CCJ was quick to point out that the views were unrepresentative and to give another side of the debate.[18]

The Church of Scotland

In 1985, the Church of Scotland issued two important reports, *Christians and Jews Today* and *Antisemitism in the World Today*.

Much of the preparatory work had been done by Jewish and Christian members of CCJ in Scotland.[19]

The United Reformed Church

In 1983, the United Reformed Church produced a very valuable study handbook called *Christians and Jews in Britain*.[20] This was the work of a group set up under the auspices of the Mission and Other Faiths Committee of the World Church and Mission department of the United Reformed Church. Some Jews and Christians of other denominations were invited to take part. Many of them and of the URC members belonged to CCJ.

The British Council of Churches

Members of CCJ have also played a part in the deliberations of the British Council of Churches and will no doubt be active in the new Council of Churches for Britain and Ireland. Rev. Kenneth Cracknell and Rev. Dr Clinton Bennett, the successive secretaries to the BCC's Committee for Relations with People of Other Faiths have attended CCJ Executive Committee meetings, as have the secretaries of the Free Church Federal Council.

WIDER INVOLVEMENT

Travel

Members of CCJ, when abroad, have also helped to make known the work. Whilst in Australia in January 1989 for the Assembly of the World Conference on Religion and Peace, I was able to meet the Archbishop of Melbourne, the Archbishop of Perth and an assistant bishop in the Diocese of Sydney. In 1990, Canon Jim Richardson was granted an audience with His Holiness the Ecumenical Patriarch Dimitrios I.

All-Christian Peace Assembly

Another aspect of CCJ's outreach has been the attendance of staff members and of officers at other international gatherings. In 1961, for example, Simpson was invited as an observer to the first All-Christian Peace Assembly in Prague and again attended the second assembly in 1964. In 1984, I was invited to the Tokyo Congress of the International Association for Religious Freedom.

CONCLUSION

CCJ has clearly made a major contribution to the spread of its ideals across the world. This has been chiefly in efforts to build up an International Council of Christians and Jews, in which Simpson and Sir Sigmund Sternberg have played a major role. CCJ too has acted as a model for similar initiatives in some other countries.

CCJ through some of its members has also contributed to changing attitudes within the Churches and the Jewish world, both by helping to formulate documents and by making them known. Many members have also been supportive of efforts in Israel to encourage dialogue and mutual understanding, especially in the support given to the Israel Interfaith Committee, to Nes Ammim and to Neve Shalom/Wahat al-Salam.[21]

10

The Issues

Amidst the wide range of the Council of Christians and Jews' concerns and activities, certain issues have been almost perennial. At the risk of some repetition, it may be helpful to look again at these recurring motifs. From this will become clear the consistency and constancy of purpose with which CCJ has dealt with them. This at first sight is surprising when the immediate memories of committee meetings may be of quite sharp disagreements. It is the more remarkable in a body drawn from a wide spectrum of both religions and with a changing membership. It suggests an underlying consensus that deserves wider acknowledgment.

ANTISEMITISM

For nearly 50 years, CCJ has struggled against prejudice, racism and discrimination. On many occasions it has protested against violations of human rights, in, for example, South Africa, Iraq and, especially, in the Soviet Union.

'The unexpected shock of the late eighties', as Dr Robert Runcie, the Archbishop of Canterbury, said to the Church of England's General Synod in July 1989, 'is to discover that all over the world – in most religions and cultures – there are those who believe they should *not* tolerate others, should avoid completely those whose beliefs they consider in error'.[1] There has recently been a disturbing increase of extremism and discrimination in many parts of the world. This suggests that the task of CCJ and other bodies is continual vigilance. In pointing to the achievements of CCJ it would be welcome to able to show how discrimination and prejudice had been reduced. Sadly, it is more like a garden. The gardener may make real improvements, but as soon as his back is turned, weeds and briars reappear. The struggle against racism and fanaticism is a relentless one and we still do not fully understand their causes.

This is particularly true of efforts to combat antisemitism. The recurrence of antisemitism in Eastern Europe and recent antisemitic outrages in Western Europe show that this sickness has not been eliminated. Whilst CCJ has been constant in its struggle against antisemitism, it is interesting that the word was not included in the original statement of aims. This is because Archbishop William Temple saw antisemitism as a manifestation of a deeper evil. 'It was a symptom, rather than the essential disease.'[2] It was, he said, 'a problem of civilisation and not only of the relationship between Jew and Christian'.[3] The need was to recall men and women to the ethical principles enshrined in the Bible.

This makes clear that the Council's work is essentially religious. Together, Jews and Christians have a responsibility to try to shape a society which is obedient to God's will, as made known in the scriptures. This is a task in which Jews and Christians are together engaged. As the Chief Rabbi, Dr Hertz, said at the preliminary meeting in 1941, Jews and Christians were being called on together 'to deal with a serious menace to the moral and spiritual life of Great Britain . . . Jews alone could do nothing'.[4]

Archbishop William Temple also recognised the difficulty of resisting antisemitism.

> One could not effectively resist such a wave of feeling as went under the name of antisemitism by merely direct opposition to it – that both called attention to it and concentrated attention upon the division which they were trying to overcome, and to some extent, like all forms of resistance stiffened that against which it was directed.[5]

Certainly, the Council has been quick to protest against blatant antisemitism. For example, it objected vigorously to *Holocaust News*, which implied that the Holocaust was a Jewish fabrication to gain sympathy for the State of Israel. It has protested again and again against antisemitic remarks in the press or in books. It has resisted attacks on *shechita*. Yet its task has been more long-term and fundamental. In 1947, Lord Reading told a meeting of representatives of Local Councils,

It has never been the prime object of this Council to enter into open conflict with the cruder forms of antsemitism, to do battle with the brawlings and bawlings of street gangs and gutter-press, but rather by promoting a more intimate and informed understanding between Christians and Jews upon the fundamental aspects of life to create a solid basis of harmony founded upon a recognition of similarities and a respect for differences.[6]

The Council has, therefore, encouraged Jews and Christians to confer on key moral matters and has pursued a wide-ranging educational programme. Initially much of the educational work was to provide basic information about the practices and beliefs of the two religious communities. Because of the large numerical superiority of Christians and therefore the Church's influence in shaping attitudes, more effort has had to be put into teaching Christians about Jews and Judaism. This has sometimes made the Council's work look unbalanced. A parallel work of helping Jews to overcome their fears and prejudices about Christianity has been pursued. In the 1980s, for example, the Council broke new ground by devoting its summer conference to a shared study of the Sermon on the Mount.

Much educational work was a matter of providing basic information. This might be in the form of leaflets about festivals or arranging a visit to a synagogue or organising a demonstration seder (passover meal). In part, this work is now also being done by others and the broadening of religious education in schools has led to a great increase in the number of books giving information about Judaism.

Indeed public ignorance of basic Christian teaching and practices is now almost as widespread, as, in the early days of CCJ, was the lack of knowledge of Judaism. As Rabbi Romain has said, it is no help in explaining the Passover to refer to the Last Supper. Many children are too ignorant of their Christian heritage to understand the reference. Once, he says, he was told that the Last Supper was the final meal before a nuclear war!

The need for clear, simple information, both through publications and audio-visual material, is still vital. It is easy to underestimate the extent of ignorance about both religions. At the last Leo Baeck conference for Christian ordinands, I asked several Christians whether they had previously visited a synagogue. Mostly, the answer was negative. As one forty-year-old student put it, 'If

I had, I would not have bothered to come' – as if one visit to a synagogue can put right centuries of Christian–Jewish hostility!

Books and talks are not enough. A deep level of relearning and discarding old attitudes is necessary. Dialogue requires an inner journey of discovery. It demands personal meeting with those of another faith and time to re-examine deeply held beliefs. Much of CCJ's most valuable work has been in providing such learning opportunities for young adults, for example in youth conferences or study tours to Israel. Sadly, this is expensive and time-consuming. In Germany, most of those training for the Christian ministry are expected to study for a year in Israel before ordination. The Churches in Britain have not been prepared to make similar resources available.

ANTI-JUDAISM

The vital importance of educating the clergy and others responsible for Christian teaching lies in the fact that one of the roots of anti-semitism is the anti-Judaism that has pervaded so much Christian teaching. It is only quite recently that the large share of responsibility which rests on the Churches for centuries of Jewish suffering has been acknowledged. Dr Robert Runcie, as Archbishop of Canterbury, took a courageous lead in confessing the Churches' shameful record.

> Without centuries of Christian antisemitism, Hitler's passionate hatred would never have been so fervently echoed . . . The travesty of Kristallnacht and all that followed is that so much was perpetrated in Christ's name. To glorify the Third Reich, the Christian faith was betrayed . . . And even today there are many Christians who fail to see it as self-evident. And why this blindness? Because for centuries Christians have held Jews collectively responsible for the death of Jesus. On Good Friday Jews have, in times past, cowered behind locked doors for fear of a Christian mob seeking 'revenge' for deicide. Without the poisoning of Christian minds through the centuries, the holocaust is unthinkable.[7]

The Lambeth Conference document, *Jews, Christians and Muslims: The Way of Dialogue*, also confesses that anti-Jewish prejudice in the Church caused untold suffering and provided the soil in which

131

'the evil weed of Nazism was able to take root and spread its poison'.[8]

Whilst most experts in the field would affirm this view, Churches are only now, in official statements, recognising their past anti-Judaism and purging their teachings and liturgies. Even so, many church members are still ignorant of these changes and even more is this the case amongst lapsed Christians, whose memory of church teaching is of what they learned in school or Sunday school perhaps 20 or maybe 40 years ago.

The traditional view was that the Jews rejected their Messiah and crucified him. God, therefore, punished the Jews, by destroying Jerusalem and scattering the Jews in exile. The Jews had forfeited the promises made to them in the *old* Covenant and these promises had been taken over by the Church, the *new* Israel, which lived by grace, not law. Often Christians came to speak of the Jews as 'children of the devil', invented infamous libels about them, made them wear distinctive dress and forced them to live in ghettos.

Different aspects of this teaching were emphasised at different times, but Christians now increasingly recognise that it is a tissue of lies. Jesus was not the Messiah of Jewish expectation. It was not 'the Jews' who crucified him. God did not abandon his covenant with Israel. Rather, it is one God of mercy and justice who speaks through the whole Bible. The Old Testament is not 'a religion of law', and in the New Testament the Pharisees are caricatured. Jesus and the first disciples were Jews, and the split between Church and Synagogue took place rather later, after the fall of Jerusalem in 70 C.E. Two creative religious traditions emerged from common roots in the Hebrew Bible: Rabbinical Judaism and the early Church, which was soon predominantly Gentile.[9]

MISSION

The touchstone of the new attitude is mission. Many Jews feel that while the Churches continue to try to convert Jews to Christianity, old attitudes have not really changed. Attempts to convert Jews seem to deny affirmations that God's covenant with Israel continues and that Jews remain God's people. Some Jews see missionary activity as even more insidious and evil than Hitler's attack on the Jewish world. That sought its physical destruction, whereas missionary activity seeks its spiritual destruction. For, if missionary activity were successful, presumably all Jews would become Christians and Judaism would disappear (although some Christians might say it had been fulfilled).[10]

From the beginning CCJ made clear that it was not a missionary or conversionist body, but its relationships with missionary organisations do not seem, until recently, to have become matters of controversy. As we have suggested, it is only really in the last 20 years that there has been a dawning recognition of Christian anti-Judaism and therefore of the theological roots of antisemitism. Equally in the 1960s and seventies CMJ and other bodies traditionally concerned with 'missions to Jews' stressed the need for a new sympathetic understanding of Judaism. The Roman Catholic order, the Sisters of Sion, completely reversed its role. Instead of seeking to convert Jews, the Sisters now try to teach Christians a new appreciation of Judaism. CMJ changed its title from 'The Church's Mission to the Jews' to 'The Church's Ministry to the Jews'. It did not abandon its claims for Jesus as the Saviour of the World and was prepared to help individuals who wished to convert, but it was not proselytising. It seems also that until the 1970s there was 'a gentleman's agreement' between CCJ and CMJ and other 'missionary' bodies not to invade each other's territory. In the 1980s, even in the Churches, gentlemanly behaviour has become less common!

Matters came to a head because of the activities of 'Jews for Jesus'. This is a movement, originating from the USA, of Jews who have come to believe that Jesus is the Messiah, but who claim that they are still Jews. They may use Hebrew for their worship and observe the Sabbath. Whilst most Jews accept, albeit reluctantly, that some Jews do convert and become Christians (and some Christians convert to Judaism), the difficulty about 'Jews for Jesus' is their claim both to believe in Jesus as Messiah and still to be Jews. Added to this, 'Jews for Jesus' have been actively seeking converts. Indeed, with the evangelical and charismatic revival in the Churches in the 1980s, several groups have become more evangelistic. This is true of CMJ, which has also given some support to 'Jews for Jesus'.

The conversionist efforts of members of 'Jews for Jesus' during the summer of 1985 disturbed the Jewish community. It was clear that the work of dialogue – and of CCJ itself – was threatened, unless church leaders distanced themselves from these efforts. After considerable consultation with the joint presidents and others, the CCJ Executive issued a statement, which expressed concern 'that

Jews, and particularly Jewish students, seem to have been singled out as targets for conversion by the missionary activities of certain Christian groups'. The statement went on to clarify the attitude of CCJ on the question of conversion.

> Throughout the centuries Christians have understood the concept of witness in various ways. Many Christians today believe it is important to develop an understanding of witness or mission which takes into account our present recognition of God's activity among other religious faiths, and of the special relationship between Christianity and Judaism. There are, however, groups who actively seek to convert Jews and who use methods which appear to be insensitive or even deceptive. Although neither CCJ nor any church organisation has power to prevent such groups working in the way they do, CCJ deplores any form of deception in evangelisation and targeting of Jews for special missionary activity.[11]

Some would have liked a more forthright repudiation of mission, but it is a concept very central to Christianity. It was therefore best to hope for a reinterpretation of the term or for more precise definition. Dr Robert Runcie, in his Sir Francis Younghusband Lecture, gave a new meaning to mission when he spoke of another goal for it 'as giving witness to the spirit of love and hope, of promoting justice and peace, sharing responsibility with others for the development of a caring society'.[12] Others, such as Lord Coggan, distinguished the word 'mission' from terms like 'proselytism', which had a sense of coercion and pressure.[13] Most importantly, however, church leaders made clear that they did not support active efforts to convert Jews.

Cardinal Hume, Archbishop of Westminster, said, on the occasion of the investiture of Sir Sigmund Sternberg as a Knight Commander of the Equestrian Order of St Gregory the Great, that he deplored attempts at 'aggressive and systematic indoctrination' particularly of Jews who were young and vulnerable. He repudiated 'ill-conceived and insensitive efforts' to convert Jews, although stating that Christians were bound to proclaim unceasingly that 'Christ is the way, the truth and the life'.[14]

The argument was renewed in the run-up to the Lambeth Conference in 1988. The content of a draft statement on Christian–Jewish relations was leaked to the press. This would have distanced the Anglican Communion from efforts to convert Jews. In the end, the statement was only able to give a presentation of the variety of views on the subject held by Anglicans.

> At one pole, there are those Christians whose prayer is that Jews, without giving up their Jewishness, will find their fulfilment in Jesus the Messiah. Indeed some regard it as their particular vocation and responsibility to share their faith with Jews, whilst at the same time urging them to discover the spiritual riches which God has given them through the Jewish faith. Other Christians, however, believe that in fulfilling the law and the prophets, Jesus validated the Jewish relationship with God, while opening up this way for gentiles through his own person. For others, the holocaust has changed their perception, so that until Christian lives bear a truer witness, they feel a divine obligation to affirm the Jews in their worship and sense of the God and Father of Jesus'.[15]

The variety of approaches prevalent in the Churches give Jews good reason to be apprehensive about the Decade of Evangelism, which started at the beginning of 1991. CCJ has been vocal in drawing these fears to the attention of church leaders, some of whom have acknowledged that the Decade is primarily addressed to members of the Churches and to lapsed Christians.[16]

ISRAEL

If the Christian members of CCJ are somewhat apologetic and defensive about the missionary activities of some of their fellow-believers, Jewish members may have a similar embarrassment about some of the actions of the Israeli government. Even so, they would often like CCJ to be more emphatic in its support for Israel. On the other hand, some Christians expect CCJ to be more critical.

Throughout its history, CCJ has made clear that it is not a political organisation. Indeed, its status as a charity precludes it from making political comment. Its primary concern is with Christian–Jewish relations in Britain and with the bearing on these of events in Israel. Israel, however, is regularly in the news. Public and Christian comment often seem to Israel's friends insensitive or unsympathetic. Many Christians visit the Holy Land as pilgrims and some return home disturbed by the plight of the Arabs.

CCJ has seen that helping Christians to appreciate the importance of Israel in Jewish self-understanding is part of its task. It has also recognised that criticism of Israel may be a cloak for anti-semitism. Further, CCJ has united Jews and Christians in Britain in support of efforts at reconciliation and peace-building in Israel.

CCJ found itself at odds, as we have seen, with the British Council of Churches over the Christian Aid video, *Palestine: Much Promised Land* and over the report *Impressions of Intifada.*[17] A meeting at the British Council of Churches' headquarters with a delegation of Palestinian Christians was also unsatisfactory.

To clarify CCJ's position and to answer charges that CCJ was merely a mouthpiece of an exclusively Jewish point of view, the chairman, Dr Edward Carpenter, wrote an open letter to the Archbishop of Canterbury. This recognises, as indeed do statements of several Churches, that for Jews, wherever they live, 'a commitment to the Land of Israel and to the existence of the State of Israel is an essential part of their own self-understanding'. If CCJ's 'writ is primarily concerned, as it must be, with British Jewry, it cannot be unaware of the profound psychological and spiritual changes consequent upon the emergence of Israel . . . Nor can CCJ be insensitive to the depth of Jewish insecurity following the Holocaust, and the insecurity of Israel, vis-à-vis its neighbouring Arab states.' In terms of political comment, the letter continues, CCJ is aware of the wide range of political views amongst both its Christian and Jewish members. It is chary of making political comment. Whilst helping Christians to understand Jewish feelings, it also tries to help Jews appreciate Christian feelings, not least in their concern for the Arab Churches and for preserving human rights wherever they are threatened.

Christians, the letter says, 'are made aware of the deep commitment to peace and human rights within Jewry, which a blanket treatment of Israelis in the press often ignores. They are also reminded of Jewish distrust of the PLO.' The letter then encourages outsiders 'to recognise that Israelis and Arabs are prisoners of a cruel history. Rather than reinforcing their resentment, it is perhaps more helpful to suggest to those who are hurt that others are hurting too. Hatred adds to the legacy of bitterness and suffering. Above all outsiders need to listen.' The letter ends by urging support for all who work for dialogue and peace.[18]

Naturally, no such statement, despite all the care put into its preparation, could satisfy everyone. Some Jews felt it should have been more emphatic in support of Israel. Some Christians would have wished for stronger affirmation of Palestinian rights to self-determination. CCJ represents a wide coalition and its primary task is to interpret Jews and Christians to each other. Whilst it has to make its own views felt, it has to avoid becoming 'a mouthpiece of any particular group or interest', or being seen as a lobby.[19] The continuing tragic situation in the Middle East makes its interpretative work ever more urgent. It is difficult in Britain to get Christians of widely different views on the situation to talk together. It is even more difficult, as CCJ found in the troubled history of its Israel Advisory Committee, to get Christians with varying views to talk together with Jews, who also hold varying views. It is even more difficult to involve Muslims. In the USA, a Religious Coalition for Peace in the Middle East has come into being, with the participation of important members of each religious community. Perhaps something similar is needed in Britain, although some multireligious conversations have taken place at the United Nations Association Religious Advisory Committee and at meetings of the UK branch of the World Conference on Religion and Peace. For, if those of different views outside the situation cannot meet and talk, there is little hope that those caught up in the situation will be able to do so.[20]

SHARED RESPONSIBILITY

In trying to encourage Jews and Christians to work together for peace and justice in the Middle East, CCJ is true to its task of seeking to enable members of both religions to witness together to the moral concerns that they share. The difficulty is that neither community is monolithic – far from it. In public discussion, for example, of attitudes to homosexuality, or on blasphemy, or even on the Nazi War Crimes Bill, there is a wide range of views in both Christian and Jewish circles.[21] In dialogue groups, it is a common experience to find that some Jews agree with some Christians whilst other Jews identify with other Christians. This makes it hard for CCJ, as such, to pontificate on such issues.

CCJ's task, perhaps, is to provide a forum where Jews and Christians of different points of view can meet and discuss current topics. In recent years, the annual CCJ Hengrave Conference has been used in this way. Instead of talks about Judaism and Christianity, the conference has focused on an important topic which is of concern to members of both religions. The 1987 conference, for example, focused on problems of family life. The speakers were Canon Frank Wright, of Manchester Extra-Mural Department, Dr Zaki Badawi, Principal of the Muslim College in London, Rev. Malcolm Weisman, an Orthodox rabbi and Rev. Io Smith, a leading member of the Black Churches. The 1989 Conference was on Ecology and Moral Problems. Rev. Dr Christopher Lamb, of Coventry Cathedral, spoke about 'Creation, Community and the Plural Society', whilst Dr Ilya Kovar, a consultant paediatrician, talked on 'Dilemmas and the Practising Doctor'. Rabbi Andrew Goldstein and Sr Margaret Shepherd spoke about environmental issues.[22] In 1990, the theme was Fundamentalism. The speakers were Dr Zaki Badawi, Rabbi Dr Dan Cohn-Sherbok of the University of Kent, Professor David Piachaud of the London School of Economics and Priscilla Chadwick, head of Bishop Ramsay School, Ruislip.[23]

By arranging such conferences – and the concerns are reflected in the programmes of local councils – CCJ makes clear that the issues are not the exclusive concern of one religious community. Indeed, public discussion is enriched by hearing various points of view. This too raises awareness of the fact that Britain has become a multiracial and multifaith society, to which people of many faith traditions have a contribution to make. The question whether, beneath this variety, there are shared moral principles on which Christians and Jews and members of other faiths agree is likely to become one on which there is increasing public debate.[24]

There are also more intimate matters of Christian–Jewish relations which merit greater attention. A number of mixed Jewish–Christian marriages take place. The leaders of both communities are aware of the difficulties that couples are likely to encounter. No encouragement is given to the couples and they seldom find it possible to arrange for a blessing of their marriage. In the Jewish world there is often considerable hostility to 'marrying out'. Yet, despite the difficultes, the couples need pastoral support and help in providing a religious upbringing for their children.

As yet only a few clergy and rabbis have given attention to this subject and CCJ, aware of the depth of feeling in some quarters, has avoided involving itself. It is, however, a matter that may need fuller and more open discussion.[25]

The same is true of the possibility of Christians and Jews being together for prayer. At the Hengrave conferences, Jewish and Christian services are held to which members of the other faith are invited as guests. These are not, however, shared worship. Some care was taken at the Clifford's Tower Commemoration in York Minster in 1990 to avoid calling it an 'interfaith service', although this term was used by some of the press. ICCJ has given more attention to this matter. At its annual colloquium, besides setting aside times for the prayers of each community, opportunity is also provided for 'shared spiritual considerations'. Great care, however, is necessary as CCJ has never wished to blur the distinctiveness of the two faiths.[26]

CONCLUSION

Old issues retain their importance, but because the Christian–Jewish relationship is a dynamic one and one set in a changing world, new topics present themselves. This is partly because as Jews and Christians get to know each other better they can touch on more sensitive matters. It is partly because their concern is for society as a whole and they have a witness to make to it together.

The title of the Council's journal is *Common Ground*. I do not see this a static concept, but rather as a description of the destination of Christian–Jewish dialogue. Whilst it is clear that in 50 years much common ground has been revealed , it is equally clear that there is much yet to discover. The first 50 years are a beginning, but there is still a great deal of the history of nineteen hundred years to unlearn, as well as a future which, with its uncertainties, will require Jews and Christians to witness together more effectively to the beliefs and values that they share.

11

The Future

Sir Sigmund Sternberg, in a lecture at Lancaster University in 1989, shared his hopes for the future of CCJ. He indicated four ways in which he would like to see its work develop. First, the new relationship between Christians and Jews needed to be more widely known. Second, members of both religions not yet engaged in dialogue should be encouraged to take part. Third, deeper theological reflection was required. Fourth, he said that his particular hope was that the two religions could do more together in the way of common action for justice and peace.[1]

MORE PEOPLE NEED TO BE EDUCATED

The need, mentioned in the first point, to make widely known what has been achieved is very important. It is the task which has always been central to the life of the Council of Christians and Jews and the International Council. The resources are inadequate and there is always more to do. Yet much has been achieved.

CCJ has taken a constant interest in efforts to ensure that a proper appreciation of Judaism and world religions is part of religious education. There are, however, twin dangers. One is that religious education will be squeezed out of a crowded timetable and the other is that the Christian 'majority' will want to use the schools to bolster Christian values. The need for adequately trained teachers – there is a shortage of Religious Education teachers and of reliable resources – will remain. Even if good material is produced, schools may not be able to afford to buy it. Religious education is often underfunded. Just as it is important that Christian children learn to appreciate Judaism, so Jewish children need to learn about Christianity. CCJ, therefore, has to continue to monitor and influence educational policy and ensure, with others, that adequate resources are available to teachers.

The importance of educating clergy and rabbis has been increasingly recognised in recent years. Their influence in shaping the attitudes of members of their congregations is considerable. They, however, have little time for inservice training, whilst the curriculum for those in training is already crowded. It is still difficult to persuade the authorities of the vital importance of the subject.

It is even more difficult to reach the 'unchurched' majority, who may well echo outdated and prejudicial teaching of a previous generation. Here, the influence of the media is considerable and CCJ has had some success in winning the sympathy of journalists and broadcasters. Symbolic events, such as the première of *Kaddish for Terezim* in Canterbury Cathedral or the interfaith gathering at York Minster 'Expressions of Heritage and Hope' in 1990, or the royal reception at St James' Palace or the receptions given by Lord Mayors of London, or the concerts planned by Paul Winner as part of the Fiftieth Anniversary programme, are very important in raising the Council's profile and in drawing attention to the new relationship between Jews and Christians which the events signify.

More immediately, although to a limited audience, CCJ achieves its educational aims through *Common Ground* and other publications. The hope is that one day *Common Ground* will be on sale at newsagents and bookstalls, as it was in its early days. There is also a strong wish, which has been echoed through the years, to increase the range and variety of CCJ publications. Now, too, CCJ has to use video and other modern methods of communication, but they are expensive.

A WIDENING INVOLVEMENT

In both communities there are groups which do not welcome the progress in Christian–Jewish relations. Those Christians who adopt a missionary approach are suspicious of dialogue, whilst their activities may make Jews suspicious of Christian intentions. There has been little creative engagement between Christians committed to dialogue and Christians, often with a traditional theological outlook, who pursue conversionist activity. There is need too for intra-Jewish discussion about the importance of dialogue. An interesting offshoot of CCJ's work has been to encourage Christians of different denominations to get to know each other and the same is true of Jews who belong to different synagogues. In Reading, the formation of a local CCJ was followed by the formation of a local Jewish Council.

A welcome trend in recent years has been the growing involvement of members of both the Orthodox Churches and the Black-led Churches in Britain. The circle of those involved in dialogue is ever widening and each new group brings a new dynamic to the process. The circle needs to be further extended.

A further development has been the growing relationship of Christian–Jewish dialogue to wider interfaith dialogue. Of particular importance has been the involvement of some Muslims in dialogue with Jews and Christians. Yet, to talk of CCJ and M (a Council of Christians and Jews and Muslims) is premature.[2] Rather, the particular relationship of Jews and Christians to each other as well as the often tragic history suggest that a council for this particular work will be needed for a long time – whatever other interfaith organisations may be required.

DEEPER THEOLOGICAL REFLECTION

Pope John Paul II, when he addressed the International Liaison Committee of Catholics and Jews in Rome in October 1985, said, 'I earnestly hope that study of and reflection on theology will become more and more a part of our exchanges for our mutual benefit even if, quite understandably, some sections of the Jewish community may still have reservations about such exchanges'.[3] Allan Brockway, who was secretary for Jewish–Christian relations at the World Council of Churches, ends a survey of their documents like this:

> Those churches which incorporate the continuing reality of the covenant between the Jewish people and God into their official theology establish a premise with far-reaching implications, both for their relations with the Jewish people and for Christian theology itself. By and large, however, the development and implementation of those implications remain in the future.[4]

There is a feeling that Christians are seriously committed to a new appreciation of Judaism, but that they have not really yet rethought traditional theology in the light of this new appreciation. For example, God's continuing covenant with the Jewish people is affirmed, but at the same time the Church speaks of Christ as the only Saviour. In the same way, still only a few Jews have studied deeply the life of Jesus. Further the dialogue itself has to include theological topics, although there has often been objection to this from Orthodox Jews.

That the theological task has still to be tackled is one reason why a Council specifically devoted to Christian–Jewish relations is required. There is some question, however, whether it is the Council's task to stimulate such theological reflection. Edward Carpenter seems to have seen this as a 'specialist area', although not one from which CCJ should be wholly left outside.[5] Lord Coggan, as chairman, appeared to give it greater priority. The theological reflection requires the resources of universities. Yet, they have to be motivated. Whilst CCJ may not be the place for original theological research, it needs to be abreast of latest developments and make them known. It is sad that resources have never been available for a research officer as well as an education officer. The importance of theology, in my view, lies in the fact that bad theology has been the cause of bad teaching which in its turn has been at the root of centuries of Christian anti-Judaism, which has caused so much Jewish suffering. Perhaps CCJ needs to consider how it can stimulate further dialogue and theological work in this field and how it can relate even more closely to institutions where such work is being done.

JUSTICE AND PEACE

If the theological task sets a particular agenda for Jews and Christians, the shared concern for justice and peace encourages Jews and Christians to work with all people of faith and good will. A certain amount is already being done through the Interfaith Network and the World Conference on Religion and Peace. Again, it would be good if the Council could afford to appoint a staff member who concentrated on the areas of social responsibility and peace and justice.

In this country the joint presidents of CCJ now meet annually to discuss social and moral issues. Even so, many would like to hear the religious leaders speaking out together more often on moral matters. This would require mechanisms for more regular consultation, and perhaps indicates another area for CCJ in facilitating such greater consultation in the coming decade.

A measure of trust and understanding has been achieved that allows Jews and Christians to address and act together on great issues like the environment, the problems of the inner cities and the search for peace and understanding, especially in the Middle East. The new relationship between Christians and Jews suggests that deeply entrenched bitterness and prejudice can, if there is good will, be overcome. If Jews and Christians have learned this lesson, they have something precious to share with all people of faith.

CONCLUSION

Edward Carpenter said in a chairman's report that one difficulty at CCJ was perhaps that it did too much. The task of rooting out all forms of discrimination and helping to build a society shaped by the ethical tradition which is shared by Jews and Christians is an enormous one and can cover a multitude of topics. With a small staff and limited resources, it has always been necessary, but difficult, to determine priorities. So much needs to be done and on that work depends in part both the prevention of future prejudice and the suffering which it can cause and also the hopes of a better world. One longs for the day when both the Christian and Jewish communities see the urgency of this task and its potential for good. Until that 'messianic time', we may not hope to finish the work, but we are not free to desist from it.

Leo Baeck, shortly before his death, said, 'I am convinced that the next great phase of the world's history will witness the emergence of a new sense of partnership between the Jewish and Christian worlds, within the kingdom and purpose of God.' With the further suggestion that the partnership will include all people of faith and goodwill, I say 'Amen.'[6]

APPENDICES

The Ten Points of Seelisberg

1. Remember that One God speaks to us all through the Old and New Testament.

2. Remember that Jesus was born of a Jewish mother of the seed of David and the people of Israel, and that His everlasting love and forgiveness embraces His own people and the whole world.

3. Remember that the first disciples, the apostles and the first martyrs were Jews.

4. Remember that the fundamental commandment of Christianity, to love God and one's neighbour, proclaimed already in the Old Testament and confirmed by Jesus, is binding upon both Christians and Jews in all human relationships, without any exception.

5. Avoid distorting or misrepresenting biblical or post-biblical Judaism with the object of extolling Christianity.

6. Avoid using the word 'Jews' in the exclusive sense of the enemies of Jesus, and the words the 'enemies of Jesus' to designate the whole Jewish people.

7. Avoid presenting the Passion in such a way as to bring the odium of the killing of Jesus upon all Jews or upon Jews alone. It was only a section of the Jews in Jerusalem who demanded the death of Jesus, and the Christian message has always been that it was the sins of mankind which were exemplified by those Jews and the sins in which all men share that brought Christ to the Cross.

8. Avoid referring to the scriptural curses, or the cry of a raging mob: 'His blood be upon us and our children', without remembering that this cry should not count against the infinitely more weighty words of our Lord, 'Father, forgive them, for they know not what they do'.

9. Avoid promoting the superstitious notion that the Jewish people are reprobate, accursed, reserved for a destiny of suffering.

10. Avoid speaking of the Jews as if the first members of the Church had not been Jews.

APPENDIX 2

The Robert Waley Cohen Lecturers

The Robert Waley Cohen Memorial Lectureship was established in 1956 as a tribute to the devoted service rendered to the Council of Christians and Jews by Sir Robert Waley Cohen. He was 'inspired by a vision of a truly democratic society in which relations between men and groups should be built upon the foundations of tolerance and mutual respect'.

1954   Sir Richard Livingstone, *Toleration in Theory and Practice*

1955   Professor Arthur Goodhart, *Tolerance and the Law*

1956   Professor Herbert Butterfield, *The Historical Development of the Principle of Toleration in British Life*

1957   Rabbi Alexander Altmann, *Tolerance and the Jewish Tradition*

1958   Rev. Dr Charles Raven, *Tolerance and Religion*

1959   Sir Isaiah Berlin, *John Stuart Mill and the Ends of Life*

1960   Dr David Stafford-Clark, *The Psychology of Persecution and Prejudice*

1961   His Excellency Abba Eban, *The Final Solution*

1962   The Archbishop of Canterbury, Dr Michael Ramsey, *The Crisis of Human Freedom*

1963   Dr David Daube, *Suddenness and Awe in Scripture*

1964   The Rt Rev. Joost de Blank, *Inter-Race Relationships*

1965   Professor Max Beloff, *The Challenge of Barbarism*

1966   Archibishop H. E. Cardinale, The Apostolic Delegate, *Religious Tolerance, Freedom and Inter-Group Relations*

1967   Professor R. J. Zwi Werblowsky, *Commitment and Indifference*

1968   Rev. Canon Henry Chadwick, *Some Reflections on Conscience: Greek, Jewish and Christian*

1970   Professor Sir Ernst Chain, *Social Responsibility and the Scientist in Modern Western Society*

1972   Professor E. Gordon Rupp, *Martin Luther and the Jews*

1974   Professor David Daiches, *The Quest for the Historical Moses*

1976   Professor Gregory Baum, *Christian Theology After Auschwitz*

1978   The Ven. Carlyle Witton-Davies, *Martin Buber and His Contribution to Jewish–Christian Understanding*

1980   Professor Uriel Tal, *Social Ethics in Modern Jewish Thought*

1982   Very Rev. D. L. Edwards, *Two Kinds of Religion Within the Jewish–Christian Tradition*

1984   Rabbi Dr Albert Friedlander, *Against the Fall of Night*

1986   Mr Alastair Hunter, *The Jewish Jesus*

1988   Dr Daniel Rossing, *The Churches in Israel*

1990   His Honour Judge Israel Finestein Q.C., *The Challenge of the Nineties*

APPENDIX 3

The Sir Sigmund Sternberg Award

The Sir Sigmund Sternberg Award is made annually as a mark of recognition and encouragement to an individual who has made a contribution to furthering Christian–Jewish relations. The nomination of the award winner is approved by the Joint President of the Council of Christians and Jews.

1979 The Venerable Carl Witton-Davies

1980 Rev. Dr I. Levy, OBE, TD

1981 Rt Rev. and Rt Hon. Lord Coggan, PC

1982 Rev. Dr Edward Carpenter, KCVO

1983 Mr Moshe Davies

1984 Canon Peter Schneider (posthumous)

1985 Rt Hon. Greville Janner, MP, QC

1986 Rt Rev. Gerald Mahon

1987 Rt Rev. James Thompson and Rabbi Hugo Gryn

1988 Dr Elisabeth Maxwell

1989 Rt Rev. Richard Harries

1990 Rabbi Dr Albert Friedlander

APPENDIX 4

Speakers at the Annual General Meetings

4 Feb. 1943   Chairman's Report by the Archbishop of Canterbury.

14 June 1944   Addresses by the Archbishop of Canterbury, the Chief Rabbi, Rt. Rev. David Matthew, Rabbi I. Brodie, Senior Chaplain to the Forces and Rev. Dr E.L. Allen on 'The Work of Local Councils'.

5 Oct. 1945   Miss Mary Trevelyan, Warden of Student Movement House and Mr Leonard Stein, President of the Anglo-Jewish Association on 'Education for Tolerance'.

4 Dec. 1946   Resolutions on Palestine and on Displaced Persons. Report on the Oxford Conference by Lord Reading.

6 Nov. 1947   Resolution on the Council's Function in Relation to Anti-semitism.

9 Dec. 1948   The Archbishop of Canterbury and Mr A.C.F. Beales. Report by Dr Pierre Visseur on 'Work in Europe'.

23 Nov. 1949   The Chief Rabbi and Professor Charles Raven, 'Group Relations: The Council's Essential Task'.

29 Nov. 1950   Countess of Listowel, the Chief Rabbi and Very Rev. W. Matthews, Dean of St Paul's, 'Religious Liberty – with Special Reference to Conditions in Eastern Europe'.

4 Dec. 1951   Professor Nevitt Sandford, Professor of Psychology, University of California, 'Recent Research into Causes of Intergroup Tensions'.

10 Dec. 1952   H.M. The Queen's patronage announced. The Chief Rabbi, Lord Pakenham, Canon Raven, 'Religious Values in Education'.

3 Dec. 1953   Rabbi Dr A. Altmann, Rev. Fr. Bernard Basset, SJ and Rev. E.H. Robertson, 'History Teaching and Community Relations'.

15 March 1955 (postponed from 9 Dec. 1954)   Very Rev. the Haham and the Bishop of Johannesburg, 'Religious Groups and Problems of Racial Tension'.

7 Dec. 1955   The Archbishop of Canterbury and the Chief Rabbi.

12 Feb. 1957   Professor Norman Bentwich, 'The Refugee: the Symbol of Our Times'.

6 March 1958   Viscount Chandos, 'Common Principles'.

25 Feb. 1959   Dr Albert de Smaele, President of the European Division of World Brotherhood, 'Cooperation Across Frontiers'.

9 March 1960   Rev. W. W. Simpson, 'Christian–Jewish Cooperation at Home and Abroad'.

1 Feb. 1961   Sir Ifor Evans, 'The Magnitude of Intolerance'.

6 March 1962   Dayan Dr Myer Lew and the Bishop of London, 'Christians and Jews in a Changing Society'.

26 March 1963   Sir John Wolfenden, 'Education in a Multi-Cultural Society'.

3 Dec. 1964   Inaugural Meeting of Reconstituted CCJ. No address.

24 March 1965   Canon G. B. Bentley of St George's, Windsor, 'Law and Society'.

17 March 1966   Ven. Martin Sullivan, Archdeacon of London, 'New Horizons in Jewish–Christian Cooperation'. (The paper was read, in the Archdeacon's absence, by Rev. W. W. Simpson).

11 May 1967 (Silver Jubilee Year)   The Archbishop of Canterbury, the Moderator of the Free Church Federal Council, Rev. H. W. Janisch, the Chief Rabbi, the Rt Rev. Christopher Butler, O.S.B., and Rev. Dr J. Fraser McLuskey.

15 May 1968   Rt Hon. Lord Segal and Ven. C. Witton-Davies, 'The Middle East and Its Impact Upon Relations Between Christians and Jews in this Country'.

21 May 1969   Mr Christopher Hollis, 'The Work of Cardinal Bea and the Implementation of the Vatican Council Declaration on the Church and the Jewish People'.

14 May 1970   The Archbishop of Canterbury, the Chief Rabbi and Dr Aubrey Vine, 'The Council of Christians and Jews – Its Realism and Relevance'.

10 June 1971   Archbishop George Appleton, Anglican Archbishop in Jerusalem, 'The Cost of Peacemaking'.

5 July 1972   Thirtieth Anniversary of the Council. The Chief Rabbi, Rev. Dr A. E. Payne, Rev. Dr J. Fraser McLuskey, the Cardinal Archbishop of Westminster. Presentation of the Buber–Rosenzweig Medal to Rabbi Dr Georg Salzberger, for founding the German-speaking Jewish community in London.

18 Sept. 1973   Professor R. J. Werblowsky, 'Jewish–Christian Relations, with particular reference to the State of Israel'.

3 July 1974   Canon Peter Hall and Rev. Dr I. Levy, 'A Branch-Eye View of the Council'.

14 Oct. 1975   The Archbishop of Canterbury, Dr Donald Coggan, 'A Christian's Tribute to Judaism'.

16 Dec. 1976   No record of an address.

15 June 1977   Extraordinary general meeting. Discussion on the Work of Local Councils, introduced by Rev. Dr T. A. Chadwick and Rev. P. Jennings.

26 Oct. 1977   No record of an address.

28 Sept. 1978   The Cardinal Archbishop of Westminster, Cardinal Hume.

9 July 1979   Lord Weidenfeld, 'The Middle East Peace. A Plea for Patience – a call for vision'.

17 July 1980   For several years, the Annual Meeting became the occasion for the presentation of the Sir Sigmund Sternberg Award. Short speeches were given by the Joint President who was making the award and by the recipient. No additional address was given.

23 June 1981

15 June 1982

22 June 1983

20 Sept. 1984   Rev. Marcus Braybrooke, 'A Shared Commitment'.

11 Sept. 1985   Dr Tudor Parfitt, 'The Jews of Ethiopia'.

30 Sept. 1986   Rev. Michael Bourdeaux of Keston College, 'Religion under Gorbachev'.

28 Oct. 1987   Dr R. Runcie, 'Drawing Closer Together'.

APPENDICES

25 Oct. 1988   Address by Cardinal Hume.

14 Nov. 1989   Dr Jonathan Sacks, 'Living Together: The Interfaith Imperative'.

14 Nov. 1990   Miss Rosemary Harthill, 'Journey Towards Judaism'.

APPENDIX 5

Local Branches in 1991

Avon
Bedford
Berkshire (Reading)
Birmingham
Blackpool
Bournemouth
Brighton and Sussex
Cambridge
Cambridge University
Cardiff
Ealing
Edgware
Edinburgh
Enfield and District
Exeter and the South-West
Finchley
Guildford
Hampstead
Harrow
Havering
Hendon and Golders Green
Hull and District
Kensington and Chelsea
Kent

Leeds
Leicester
Manchester
Marylebone
Merseyside
The North East
North London
Northampton and District
Nottingham
Oxford
Radlett and District
Redbridge
Sheffield
South London
Suffolk and North Essex
Southend
Southport
Stanmore
Staines
West of Scotland
North West Middlesex (Wembley)
Willesden
Wimbledon

Notes

Dates refer to the Minutes of meetings of the CCJ Council or Executive Committee. CG is an abbreviation for *Common Ground*, the Council's journal. Details of books are given when the first reference is made to them.

1. PREWAR PREPARATIONS

1. From an undated document circulated amongst a group of interested Jews. In the Simpson archives.
2. *The Promise*, No. 26, July 1925, pp. 2–3.
3. Ibid., p. 3.
4. Quoted from W. W. Simpson, *Where Two Faiths Meet*, CCJ 1955, pp. 15–16.
5. Ibid., p. 16.
6. *In Spirit and in Truth, Aspects of Judaism and Christianity*, Edited for the Society of Jews and Christians by G.A.Yates. Hodder & Stoughton, 1934, p. xii.
7. Letter, 9 Dec. 1930, Parkes to Hoffmann. Parkes Archives, quoted by Theodore C. Linn in an unpublished essay, 'From Conversion to Cooperation; James Parkes' Call to Christian Conscience'.
8. Ibid.
9. *Jewish Chronicle*, 28 Aug. 1981, quoted in a letter from Mr Sidney Sugarman.
10. Robert Andrew Everett, 'James Parkes: Historian and Theologian of Jewish Christian Relations', Columbia University Ph.D Thesis, 1983. From the Abstract.
11. *Anti–Semitism in the World Today*, Church of Scotland Board of World Mission and Unity, 1985, Appendix VIII, p. 68.
12. Cyclostyled Memorandum by W. W. Simpson.
13. John Presland, *A Great Adventure. The Story of the Refugee Children's Movement*, Gladys Benedit, July 1944, pp.7–8.
14. Christopher Howse, 'Christians and Jews' in *The Tablet*, 20 April 1985, p. 392.
15. W. W. Simpson, *The Christian and the Jewish Problem*, Epworth, 1939, p. 16.
16. Ibid., p. 19.
17. Ibid., p. 21.
18. Ibid., p. 24.

2. THE BEGINNINGS

1. James Parkes, *Voyages of Discovery*, Gollancz, 1969, p. 174. W. W. Simpson, Lecture to the Jewish History Society, 17 March 1982.
2. Memo of Meeting on 19 Nov. 1941, p. 4.
3. Ibid., p.1.
4. Ibid., pp. 2–3.
5. Ibid., pp. 5–6.
6. Minutes of this meeting are in the Council Minutes, Book I.
7. 8 July 1942.
8. Report of an Extraordinary Meeting, 20 Feb. 1946.
9. 8 Sept. 1942.
10. Appendix to Minutes of 21 Sept. 1942.
11. *Jewish Chronicle*, 2 Oct. 1942, p. 8.

3. EARLY YEARS

1. 3 Dec. 1942.
2. 7 Dec. 1942.
3. AGM, 4 Feb. 1943.
4. 18 Nov. 1943.
5. Attached memorandum to minutes of 16 May 1944. See also the AGM, June 1944.
6. F. A. Iremonger, *William Temple*, OUP, 1948, p.565.
7. Ibid., p. 566.
8. Ibid., p. 567.
9. Ibid., p. 567.
10. Ibid., p. 567.
11. 10 Sept. 1947.
12. AGM, 4 Dec. 1946.
13. 7 May 1946 and 3 July 1946.
14. 9 Nov. 1948.
15. AGM, 23 Nov. 1949.
16. 5 Aug. 1943.
17. 6 May 1943.
18. Meeting of representatives of Local Councils, 17 June 1947.
19. *CG*, Nov/Dec. 1946, p.3.
20. AGM, 29 Nov. 1950.
21. Council Meeting, Dec. 1943.
22. AGM, 23 Nov. 1949.
23. See my *Pilgrimage of Hope*, (SCM Press, forthcoming) and W. W. Simpson and Ruth Weyl, *The International Council of Christians and Jews: A Brief History*, ICCJ, 1988, pp. 22–4 and see below, pp. 118–19.
24. 4 April 1944.
25. Memo in AGM Minutes Book, 17 June 1947.
26. AGM, 20 Feb. 1946.

27. *CG*, 1958/2, p. 5.
28. Henry Carter's Chairman's Report, AGM, 23 Nov. 1949.

4. CATHOLIC WITHDRAWAL AND RETURN

1. Memo 5 Nov. 1954.
2. Letter from Cardinal Griffin, 6 Nov. 1954.
3. Letter from Archbishop Fisher, 11 Nov. 1954.
4. Letter from Cardinal Griffin, 22 Nov. 1954.
5. Memo 6 Dec. 1954.
6. Memo, 'Summary of Press reports on Roman Catholic Resignations', 11 Jan. 1955.
7. *The Universe*, 4 Nov. 1990.
8. *Catholic Herald*, 3 July 1981 and Letter of 4 Sept. 1981. For further reference to World Brotherhood see below, Chapter 9.
9. Letter of Dr Pierre Visseur, 5 Oct. 1981.
10. Letter of 19 Nov. 1947.
11. See my forthcoming *Pilgrimage of Hope*.
12. *The Tablet*, 27 April 1985.
13. Ibid. and letter of W.W. Simpson, 20 May 1956.
14. Letter of W.W. Simpson, 14 March 1957.
15. Letter to Cardinal Lienart, 4 May 1961.
16. ATV, 17 Dec. 1961.
17. *Catholic Times*, 16 March 1962.
18. AGM, March 1964.
19. *The Tablet*, 18 Dec. 1982.
20. CCJ Circular to Local Councils, 1 Jan. 1967.
21. Memo 10 Jan. 1969.
22. Letter from Witton-Davies, 4 Feb. 1969.

5. THE SIMPSON YEARS

1. *CG* 1975/1, p.15.
2. 12 June 1957.
3. F.W. Dillistone, *Charles Raven: Naturalist, Historian, Theologian.* Hodder & Stoughton, 1974, and review in *CG* 1975/1, pp. 17–18.
4. Charles Raven, *Tolerance and Religion*, 1958 Waley Cohen Lecture, CCJ, p.8.
5. Ibid, p.16.
6. 20 June 1956.
7. 27 July 1967.
8. 7 Jan. 1953.
9. 23 Sept. 1953 and 21 Oct. 1953.
10. 7 May 1964, 29 Feb. 1968, 19 Jan. 1971, 23 May 1972.
11. 1955 AGM; 9 Dec. 1971.
12. 28 Jan. 1969 and 28 Oct. 1969.
13. Nov. and Dec. 1961, 13 Dec. 1961.
14. 13 Dec. 1961.

15. 16 Jan. 1962.
16. 31 March 1971, 29 July 1971.
17. 18 Sept. 1958.
18. Ibid.
19. 7 June 1962, 18 June 1962.
20. 25 June 1968.
21. 25 Sept. 1962. 23 Oct. 1962.
22. 13 Dec. 1962, 12 Dec. 1968; Joan Lawrence, *Some Aspects of Shechita*, CCJ 1971 and 1985 (rvd.)
23. 5 March 1970.
24. 6 Nov. 1968.
25. 23 Sept. 1954, 19 July 1956, 15 Jan. 1957.
26. The discussion about admission to public schools was mostly in 1954. The article by Albert Polack was in the Autumn 1954 issue of *CG*.
27. The discussion about Carmel College was on 16 Jan. 1961.
28. 25 June 1968.
29. 25 May 1961, 26 July 1961, 16 Jan. 1962.
30. See Appendix One.
31. 15 Sept. 1960.
32. Attached to Minutes for 5 March 1970.
33. 7 April 1964.
34. 31 March 1971.
35. George Appleton, *Unfinished*, Collins, 1990, pp.136–7.
36. *Facing Realities*, CCJ 1969.
37. 13 July 1960.
38. Attached to the minutes for 1970. See also *CG* 1970/1 Editorial and article by Sister Louis Gabriel. See also *CG* 1990/3. In the *Jewish Chronicle* for 30 Mar. 1990, Rev. Peter Jennings is reported as saying, 'All existing texts and alterations to the play should be buried. It is the only honourable thing to do.'
39. 11 Feb. 1953.
40. 21 Oct. 1953.
41. 5 Nov. 1956.
42. 2 Dec. 1958.
43. 19 Feb. 1959. The leaflet of the Committee for Inter-Faith Understanding in Israel is attached to the minutes.
44. *Jewish Chronicle* obituary, 14 Aug. 1981.
45. *CG*, Summer 1990.
46. Letter of Dr Warhaftig, Minister of Religious Affairs, to WWS, 15 May 1964, attached to minutes for 17 June 1964.
47. 10 March 1955.
48. 3 April 1963. The document containing the proposals is in the CCJ file at the *Jewish Chronicle* Library.
49. 27 Nov. 1956.
50. 28 March 1957.
51. Report attached to the minutes of 23 June 1970.
52. *CG*, 1975/1, p.16.
53. *CG*, 1974/3, pp.5–10.
54. *Jewish Chronicle*, 29 Aug. 1987.
55. *Theology*, Sept. 1987, pp.382–3
56. *CG* 1974/3, p.21.

6. THE STRUGGLE TO SURVIVE

1. Annual Report 1975–6, *CG*, Autumn 1976, p.4.
2. Ibid, p.11.
3. Chairman's Introduction, Ibid, p.10.
4. *CG*, 1978/1, p.3 and p.19.
5. AGM, 1978. *CG*, 1978/4, p.5.
6. Annual Report, 1977–8. *CG* 1978/3, p.7.
7. *CG*, 1974/4, p.14.
8. 'The Chairman Speaks', *CG* 1979/1, p.8.
9. Minutes of AGM, 22 June 1983.
10. Editorial, *CG* 1979/1, p.1
11. *CG*, 1980/2, p.4.
12. *CG*, 1980/4, pp.12–13.
13. *CG*, 1979/1, p.3.
14. *CG*, 1979/2, p.19. and Lord Weidenfeld's address to AGM, 1979. *CG* 1979/3, p.15.
15. Executive minutes, 6 Dec. 1973 and minute 959, of meeting on 7 Feb. 1974.
16. Executive minutes, 4 Dec. 1979.
17. Executive minutes, 17 July 1980.

7. EXPANDING HORIZONS

1. Memorandum, June 1984.
2. See the article by Pauline Smith in *CG*, 1991/1.
3. *Clifford's Tower Commemoration Programme*, B'nai B'rith and CCJ, 1990 p.85.
4. *CG*, 1990/2, p.9.
5. *CG*, 1988/4 and *Remembering for the Future*, the conference papers, Pergamon Press, Maxwell Macmillan, 1989.
6. Emil Fackenheim, *The Jewish Bible After the Holocaust: A Re-reading*, Manchester University Press, 1991. Geoffrey Wigoder, *Jewish–Christian Relations Since the Second World War*, Manchester University Press, 1988.
7. *CG*, 1989/1 and Kristallnacht Memorial Meeting, pamphlet, CCJ 1990, pp. 2–6.
8. Ibid, pp.7–8.
9. Ibid, p.12.
10. Memorandum agreed June 1984.
11. See below, Chapter 8.
12. Memorandum, June 1984.
13. See below, pp. 135–7.
14. Albert Friedlander, *A Thread of Gold*, SCM Press, 1990, p.112.
15. Ibid., p.111.
16. See below, pp. 132–5.

17. *Palestine: The Much Promised Land*, Christian Aid Video, 1988. *Impressions of Intifada*, British Council of Churches, 1989.
18. Executive minutes, 26 June 1990.
19. *CG*, 1990/2, p.11. See below, pp.135–6.
20. CCJ Tour in *CG*, 1990/3 and Young Adults Tour, *CG*, 1990/2.
21. *CG*, 1990/3 and 1991/1 and Eric Moonman, 'Why Christians must speak out against antisemitism', *The Times*, 17 Dec. 1990.

8. LOCAL COUNCILS

1. 4 April 1944.
2. Memorandum in AGM minutes book, 17 June 1947 and see below, pp. 108–9.
3. Memorandum attached to the minutes, 16 Jan. 1962.
4. Aide mémoire of a meeting of Representatives of Local Councils, 29 Jan. 1969.
5. Letter of Mrs Zoe Young to Simpson, 11 Aug. 1970.
6. Circular letter of P. Jennings, 16 April 1975.
7. Letter of Dr I. Levy, 16 May 1975.
8. 24 Oct. 1984 and 21 Sept. 1987.
9. 17 March 1987.
10. 8 June 1988.
11. 20 Sept. 1989.
12. *CG*, 1990/3, p.43.
13. Address to Council, 14 June 1944.
14. Minutes of a Special Meeting held on 17 June 1947.
15. Minutes of the meeting of Local Council representatives, held on 5–6 March, 1962.
16. The several files of correspondence with Nottingham are part of the CCJ archive, housed at the Parkes Library.
17. *CG*, 1991/1.

9. INTERNATIONAL INVOLVEMENT

1. William W. Simpson and Ruth Weyl, *The International Council of Christians and Jews*, ICCJ, p.20.
2. See my *Pilgrimage of Hope: A History of the Interfaith Movement*, SCM Press, forthcoming.
3. Minutes of Extraordinary General Meeting, 13 March 1944.
4. Executive Committee Statement, May 1944. Attached to minutes of AGM, 14 June 1944.
5. See note 3.
6. Simpson and Weyl, p.23, n.1.
7. *Freedom, Justice and Responsibility*, Conference Report, CCJ, 1946.
8. See Appendix One.
9. Simpson and Weyl, ICCJ, p.32, n.1.
10. Ibid., p.35.
11. Ibid., pp.66–72.
12. See especially *Ecumenical Considerations on Jewish–Christian Dialogue*, 1982, the *Sigtuna Consultation Report*, 1988, and *The Theology of the*

Churches and the Jewish People. Statements by the World Council of Churches and its Member Churches, Ed. Alan Brockway, 1988, all published by the WCC. See also my *Time to Meet*, SCM Press, 1990, pp. 23–9.

13. Gerhard Riegner, *Fifteen Years of Catholic Jewish Dialogue 1970–1985*, Libraria Editrice Vaticana, Rome 1988, p.278. See also Geoffrey Wigoder, *Jewish–Christian Relations since the Second World War*, my *Time to Meet*, and the collections of documents edited by Helga Croner, *Stepping Stones to Christian–Jewish Relations* and *More Stepping Stones to Christian–Jewish Relations*, Stimulus Books, 1977 and 1985.
14. *CG*, 1991/1.
15. *Christian–Jewish Relations*, 14/1, March 1981, *passim*.
16. *Christian–Jewish Relations*, 20/3, Autumn 1987, pp. 39–41. Anglican–Jewish Consultation.
17. 'Jews, Christians and Muslims: The Way of Dialogue' in *The Truth Shall Make You Free: The Lambeth Conference, 1988*; The Anglican Consultative Council, 1989, Appendix, p.229.
18. Anglican Consultative Council paper, Jan. 1988.
19. *Christians and Jews Today* and *Anti-Semitism in the World Today*, Church of Scotland Board of World Mission and Unity, 1985, Appendices VII and VIII, pp. 55ff.
20. *Christians and Jews in Britain*, United Reformed Church, 1983.
21. The Israel Interfaith Committee, Tchernichovsky Street 5, PO Box 7739, Israel; Friends of Nes Ammim, c/o Rev. Peter Jennings, Whitechapel Mission, 212 Whitechapel Road, London E1 1BJ; British Friends of Neve Shalom, 24 Culverlands Close, Green Lane, Stanmore, Middx HA7 3AG; Helen Silman-Cheong, *Wellesley Aron – Rebel with a Cause: A Memoir*, Vallentine, Mitchell, 1991.

10. THE ISSUES

1. *CG*, 1989/2, p.3.
2. Report of Conference on Jewish–Christian Relations, 19 Nov. 1941, cyclostyled, p.1.
3. Ibid.
4. Ibid., p.2.
5. Ibid., p.1.
6. Meeting of the National and Local Councils, 17 June 1947.
7. *CG*, 1989/1, pp.21–2.
8. 'Jews, Christians and Muslims: The Way of Dialogue', p. 303.
9. See my *Time to Meet*, pp.105–6.
10. Ibid., p.96.
11. CCJ Statement on Missionary Activity, 13 March 1986.
12. *Time to Meet*, p.98.
13. Ibid., p.99.
14. *The Times*, 5 March 1986.
15. *CG*, 1988/4, p.7.
16. See my article in *The Expository Times*, March 1991 and my letter in *The Times*, 5 Jan. 1991. See also *CG*, 1991/2.
17. See above p.144. *Palestine: The Much Promised Land*, Christian Aid video,

1988. *Impressions of Intifada*, British Council of Churches, 1989.
18. *CG*, 1990/2, p.11.
19. Ibid.
20. The US Interreligious Coalition for Peace in the Middle East, Greene and Westview, 3rd Floor, Philadelphia PA 19119; The World Conference on Religion and Peace, 14 Chemin Auguste-Vilbert, CH 1218 Grand Saconnex, Geneva, Switzerland. The Co–chairman of the UK Chapter is Rabbi Dr Albert Friedlander.
21. *The Independent* series of articles 'Faith and Reason' on homosexuality, Sept. 1987; on blasphemy, *CG*, 1990/2, pp.5–6.; on Nazi War Crimes, *CG* 1990/3 and 1991/1.
22. *CG*, 1990/1.
23. *CG*, 1990/3.
24. See Dr Jonathan Sacks' Reith Lectures, *The Persistence of Faith*, Weidenfeld & Nicolson, 1991, and my review of his *Tradition in an Untraditional Age*, Vallentine Mitchell, 1989, in *CG* 1991/1; also Hans Küng's *Global Ethics*, SCM Press 1991.
25. Rabbi Jonathan Romain, *CG* 1989/1 and *Manna*, 1989, pp.18–19.
26. See my background paper 'Reconciliation Between Jews and Christians Through Common Prayer' in *From The Martin Buber House*, ICCJ, No. 10, 1985/6, pp.49–52.

11. THE FUTURE

1. *CG*, 1990/1, p.5.
2. *CG*, 1990/3 and 1991/1.
3. *Fifteen Years of Catholic–Jewish Dialogue, 1970–1985*, p.320.
4. Allan Brockway in *The Theology of the Churches and the Jewish People*, p.186. See also David Novak, *Jewish–Christian Dialogue: A Jewish Justification*, Oxford University Press, 1989.
5. *CG* 1989/1.
6. Leo Baeck, quoted in the Memorandum of the Manchester Council on a World Conference. See also Hans Küng, *Global Ethics*, SCM Press, 1991.

Index

of personal names mentioned in the text

INDEX